CFDs Made Simple

A straightforward guide to contracts for difference

Peter Temple

HARRIMAN HOUSE LTD

3A Penns Road
Petersfield
Hampshire
GU32 2EW
GREAT BRITAIN

Tel: +44 (0)1730 233870
Fax: +44 (0)1730 233880
Email: enquiries@harriman-house.com
Website: www.harriman-house.com

First published in Great Britain in 2009
Copyright © Harriman House Ltd

The right of Peter Temple to be identified as Author has been asserted
in accordance with the Copyright, Design and Patents Act 1988.

ISBN: 978-1906659-08-0

British Library Cataloguing in Publication Data
A CIP catalogue record for this book can be obtained from the British Library.

Printed and bound by the CPI Group, Antony Rowe

About the author

Peter Temple has been working in and writing about financial markets for the last 36 years. After an 18 year career in fund management and stockbroking, he became a full-time writer in 1988.

His articles appear in the *Financial Times*, *Investors Chronicle* and a range of other publications. Peter is a regular contributor to *Interactive Investor*. He has written more than a dozen books about investing, mainly aimed at private investors.

He and his wife live in part of a converted bobbin mill in the Lake District National Park.

Contents

Preface

What this book covers

This book is about using contracts for difference (CFDs) as part of your overall investment strategy. CFDs are available in a wide range of instruments, including shares, bonds, and commodities, and for securities in both the UK and many other international markets. Most of the examples in this guide relate to application of CFD trading with reference to the UK equity market.

Who the book is for

CFDs can be used both by traders who want an easy-to-use highly geared investment medium, and by investors who wish to invest using the minimum of capital, or else to use CFDs as a means of hedging an already sizeable investment portfolio.

This book is intended for existing private investors considering using CFDs as part of their investment strategy, or those who may have begun trading CFDs but wish to acquire a more in-depth understanding of the market. We assume a certain amount of knowledge and experience on the part of readers. CFD brokers will not normally take on clients unless they have substantial capital at their disposal and can demonstrate past experience in trading and investing.

How the book is structured

After a brief introduction, the book looks at the basic concepts that would-be users need to understand before embarking on CFD trading. It then goes on to look at how CFDs work, focusing on the 'rules of the road' to observe when trading them, and on the risks involved. The guide then looks at the mechanics of CFD dealing, including the use of stop-loss orders. It then covers trading strategies, money management disciplines and using technical analysis to time trades. A final section looks at further reading and other relevant resources.

The risks involved

We cannot stress too strongly that trading CFDs involves gearing and high levels of risk. If a trade goes wrong, you may lose many times more than you have initially invested. We strongly recommend that all CFD traders use stop-loss orders to limit risk, and not embark on trading before they understand the true nature of the risks involved. Neither the author nor the publishers can in any way be held responsible for any losses you may incur as a result of basing your trading on any of the material or ideas in this book.

Risk warning

No responsibility for loss incurred by any person or corporate body acting or refraining to act as a result of reading material in this book can be accepted by the Publisher or the Author.

The information provided by the Author is not offered as, nor should it be inferred to be, advice or recommendation to readers, since the financial circumstances of readers will vary greatly and investment or trading behaviour which may be appropriate for one reader is unlikely to be appropriate for others.

1
Introduction

The D-word

This book is about an investment medium known as contracts for difference (CFDs). CFDs are part of a wider group of investment products known as derivatives. These are so called because their value *derives* from the movement in price of an underlying asset or security. Apart from CFDs, which are relatively recent in origin, other derivatives include venerable products like futures and options, which have existed for centuries in one form or another, and spread betting and warrants.

After the events of October 2008, when the financial system came close to meltdown as a result (arguably) of the activities of professional derivatives traders in the banking system, investors might be forgiven for wondering whether or not they should have anything to do with this particular 'D-word'.

Debacles like this are not new. In the 1990s Barings was brought down by ill-judged derivatives trades made by Nick Leeson. The derivatives losses at the hedge fund Long Term Capital Management provoked a crisis of confidence in the financial system in 1998. And the fortunes made and, more particularly lost, on derivatives date back at least as far as the mania for tulip bulbs in Holland in the 16th century.

This history might suggest that caution is warranted when using them. But employed in the correct way, derivatives can function as insurance rather than as a means of highly geared speculation.

In other words, the D in derivatives needn't stand for danger. This book is here to help you understand CFDs and to use them in a way that suits your investing style. Used properly they can help improve your returns and control the risks that you run.

Many investors lost plenty of money through investing in equities in the later stages of the bull market that ended in early 2000. If they had used some of the tools we'll explore in this book, they could have limited and even offset their losses.

That's why CFDs are worth taking seriously.

Are we set for a long period of modest returns?

Though I've researched the equity market in one form or another for well over thirty-five years, I still find it hard to pinpoint exactly when a new uptrend or downtrend in the market will begin. In fact no one really knows.

Over long periods, as the table later in this chapter shows, the returns from equities as a whole are relatively modest and the market is characterised by swings around a long-term average. If prices get too far above or below this ultra long-term trend, eventually it corrects.

This is known as 'reversion to the mean'. It might mean that, while shares do not fall any more than they have, there is a period of further underperformance to make up for the good times investors have, on the whole, enjoyed in the long bull phase that ran from the early 1980s until 2000.

If so, the best that investors can hope for from their holdings in shares or bonds is single digit percentage gains on average, combined with volatility. Some years will be good and some will be bad. Percentage changes and swings from peak to trough and back again could be quite substantial. This is an entirely normal pattern.

The bull market of the 1990s was the exception, the like of which had not been seen since the 1920s. The 1920s bull market itself ended in a systemic banking crisis and the Great Depression. After the 1980s and 1990s bull market, and the recent crash, a repetition of gains like this will not be seen for another generation or two.

Excluding bubbles, the normal market pattern is for bull markets to last just short of four years and for bear markets to be nasty, but brief, perhaps lasting just under two years. There have also been (sometimes quite long) periods during which the markets have gone sideways, as the table shows.

The message is that the returns experienced in equities for much of the 1990s and between 2003 and 2007 were a flash in the pan. Long-term real gains from equities are almost always a single figure percentage. In stagnant markets they are likely to be plus or minus low single figures. And if returns over the last few years have been above average, then that suggests there's a strong possibility of below average returns for the next few. Some of this reversion to the mean has already been seen. Even at its worst in October and November 2008, the FTSE 100 index was still above the low seen five years previously in July 2003.

So, history tells us that just repeating the strategies we used in the 1980s and 1990s bull market, or indeed more recently, might not work in any new stock market era that's maybe neither bull nor bear market, but something in between the two.

One reason for this is that the millions of private investors who have become progressively more actively involved in the market since the privatisations of the 1980s will have been scarred for life by their experiences of the market that culminated in the banking crisis of October 2008. There is an old saying that a deep bear market breaks the heart of a generation of investors.

If so, investors may become much more interested in buying and holding safer investments like government bonds, or keeping their money in bullion, collectibles and cash deposits.

But professional investors will still be investing in shares and markets will rise as prosperity returns. The fact that many private investors are shunning the market is a reason for the astute ones that remain to earn better than average returns.

We could of course go back to the fundamental tools and theories of earlier eras when more stable, range-bound markets were the norm. But wacky theories like Gann, Elliott Wave, or even astrology are probably not the real solution to the problem of coping with markets like this.

Table 1.1: Barclays Capital's Equity-Gilt Study, Annual real returns

Period	Equities(%)	Gilts(%)	Cash(%)
1947-52	-4.0	-0.9	-4.8
1960-62	-2.4	3.5	1.2
1969-73	-4.1	-4.7	-1.6
1975-81	4.9	-0.4	-1.0
1987-90	2.8	-0.9	5.4
3 yrs to 2005	14.8	2.8	1.6
10yrs to 2005	4.2	5.7	2.8
20yrs to 2005	6.7	6.2	3.9
50yrs to 2005	7.0	2.3	2.0
1900-2005	5.2	1.2	1.0
2007	1.0	1.2	1.8

Source: Barclays Capital Equity-Gilt Study 2008 Edition

In this new environment, it may pay to look more closely at some of the tools that are available to help our most basic of investment decisions. We should not exclude using new techniques and investment products that have been devised from the mid-1970s onwards, including CFDs. They can help boost returns in what may be a particularly unrewarding period for 'normal' investment techniques. They can also help us to get the maximum returns from scarce capital and hedge our bets where necessary.

What are the new techniques we need to survive?

The preserve of well-heeled City punters, CFDs and spread betting originated in the 1970s and 1980s. Trading began with a limited range of instruments.

As a digression, IG Index, one of the largest CFD and spread betting firms, was so called because the initials stood for Index Gold. In 1975, when it began life, its aim was to allow investors, mainly professionals, to speculate on the gold price. It, and other firms, also began offering spread betting in the major indices, and City insiders had a field day using this method to back their judgement.

In the bear market from 2000 to 2003, CFD and spread betting firms (most spread betting outfits have a CFD arm, and vice versa) were particularly active marketers. Spread betting and CFDs became and have remained popular. One reason is the ease with which they enable investors to speculate on a fall in the price of a share or index.

The number of private investors with, for example, spread betting accounts has increased dramatically. Contracts for difference have grown up in much the same way.

They are aimed at the more serious and well-heeled punter. Both products offer investors a one-stop shop for a range of investments. They enable trading within tightly controlled risk limits in the form of *guaranteed stop-losses* (a service for which few conventional brokers have any appetite), no stamp duty and, in the case of spread betting, no CGT either.

Why do we need them?

This book is about CFDs rather than spread betting. But both CFDs and spread betting allow us to address what are likely to be some of the main features of the era that we find ourselves in right now. I've reduced these to some key bullet points illustrating investors' needs in the markets we may face for the next few years:

- We need to be **nimble**. Buy and hold investing on its own is not going to yield us decent returns.

- We need, if we can, to have a means of getting money into and out of the index **quickly at a low cost** and with the minimum of fuss.

- We need to be able to **make money if the market is falling** as well as if it is rising. For a few years yet the market will be switching between periods of elation and depression, and we need to be able to capitalise on those swings.

- Since markets may be volatile, we need ways of **controlling our risk**.

- We need to try and **magnify our returns** wherever possible, because overall returns are likely to be low. This means using our judgement. CFDs can help to produce bigger returns when the time is right.

These are the topics we aim to cover in this short book. We'll look at how they work, when and when *not* to use them, how to deal in them, who to deal with, where to get information about them, and why they make sense for managing our investments.

2

Basic Concepts

A ll derivatives, including CFDs, rest on some basic concepts that we need to understand thoroughly before getting involved in them. They are the building blocks we need to master. So let's start right off by listing them. Derivatives like CFDs are a lot easier to understand if you look at their component parts first.

So let's have a look at each of these ideas in turn.

[When you reach the end of the chapter it might be worth re-reading it to make sure you've got these ideas firmly planted in your mind.]

Table 2.1: Basic components of derivatives

Building block	Relevant to
Underlying	All derivatives, including CFDs
Contracts	All derivatives, including CFDs
Cash settlement	All derivatives, including CFDs
Gearing	All derivatives, including CFDs
Hedging	Futures, options, CFDs, spread betting and options
Indexes	Index futures and options, CFDs, spread betting
Margin	All futures, some option trades, CFDs, spread betting
Short selling	All futures, CFDs, spread betting

Underlying

We will be using the term *underlying* as a noun rather than an adjective quite a few times in the book. Let's start by defining exactly what it means. Quite simply, the *underlying* is the share, index, commodity or other instrument on which a CFD or other derivative contract is based. The price of the derivative is *derived from* the price of the underlying. Just to confuse matters, the market price of the underlying is sometimes also referred to as the *cash* or *spot* price.

For example, in the case of a Vodafone CFD the *underlying* is Vodafone shares and the *cash* price is the price of Vodafone shares (as distinct from the price of the Vodafone CFD).

Key concept

The price of the derivative is determined by the price of the underlying. Using the word *underlying* is a reference to the share, index, or commodity on which the derivative is based.

Contracts

The next concept to get your head round is the idea that you are buying and selling a *contract* rather than an *asset*. This is fundamental to almost all derivatives. CFDs are no exception.

When you buy a share you own an asset: a small piece of a listed company. Similarly, if you buy a unit trust, you have a stake in the fund's portfolio.

CFDs and other derivatives are different.

Here, you are entering into an *agreement*, or a contract. It has certain rights and obligations attached. In other words, if you buy or sell a derivative you are in fact making an agreement that holds good until you *close* the trade. So you are trading a *promise* to do something, not dealing in the underlying item on which the promise is based.

That contract can take many forms. It can simply be a promise to buy (or sell) a fixed quantity of something at a specified time in the future, paying or receiving today's price for it. This is called a *future*.

But you might want to pay to have the *choice* of either buying (or selling) something *or not* at a fixed price in the future. In other words you want to have the *option* of buying (or selling) it. But if it isn't in your interest to do so, you don't want to be forced into making the purchase (or sale). This is called an *option*.

A CFD is neither of these things. It is (in the jargon) a *total return equity swap*, in which you are paying a modest down payment to get 100% of the economic exposure (i.e. the gains or losses that might occur) in the price of a share or other underlying. The down payment (called *margin*) represents a deposit to ensure that you keep your side of the bargain if the price moves in the opposite direction to what you expect.

Key concept

A CFD is not a claim on an underlying asset, like a share or bond, but simply a paper contract. Because it represents an agreement rather than ownership, it is more flexible to trade.

Cash settlement

Many derivatives involve having something physical to deliver. For example, a futures contract on wheat may involve the physical delivery of tonnes of wheat when the contract expires.

But many more derivatives are based on something less tangible. In the financial futures market, for example, there are contracts based around interest rates and around long-term government bond prices. There are futures and options, and spread betting and CFD contracts based around stock market indices.

In these cases it is either impossible or impractical to have physical delivery of the underlying interest rate, bond or share index. Imagine, for example, in the case of a stock market index, having to assemble the 100 shares in the FTSE 100 in the exact proportions and at the exact price they were at the time the contract was settled. It just wouldn't work.

So an alternative has been devised. For many derivatives it is possible simply to settle in cash for the difference between your buying and selling price. You simply pay or receive the difference between the prices at which you open and close your trade, multiplied by the size of the contract. This might be, for example, the number of shares involved, if you have been trading a CFD in shares.

For example, if you buy five Vodafone CFDs when you come to sell them settlement will involve only a transfer of cash – you will not be involved in any transfer of Vodafone shares.

There are other aspects to trading CFDs, but cash settlement is an important underlying principle.

Gearing

Most ways of dealing in derivatives involve gearing. The gearing is either inherent to the derivative itself (as with options) or, as with CFDs, created because of the way they are traded.

Gearing is both an attraction and a danger. The gearing element in a CFD comes about through the fact that you trade by putting up a down payment (called *margin*). If the price moves up, the effect of this feature is to gear up the return on your capital.

It's rather like buying a house with a mortgage. It's fine if the price goes in your favour – your equity in the house multiplies. But if you get it wrong, you can end up with large negative equity.

When you are trading derivatives you need to take care. The gearing works both ways. You could double your money, or be wiped out, by a small move up or down in the underlying price.

Example – Gearing in CFDs

You buy some Vodafone CFDs and your broker asks you to put up £1000 (this £1000 is the margin to cover the position). If the underlying Vodafone shares increase by 10% and you sell your CFDs, your profit on the trade could be around £660. That's a 66% return on the original £1000 you put up; which is 6 times more than the 10% increase in the underlying Vodafone shares.

Nice. But, if the shares had fallen 10%, then you would have *lost* around £660. In other words, a modest 10% fall in the underlying Vodafone shares would have lost you two thirds of your initial £1000 investment.

This might seem risky. But there are ways of trading that allow you to avoid, or limit, the risk that this gearing implies. The easiest way to avoid it is to make sure, when you deal in CFDs, that you reduce the size of the stake accordingly.

If, for example, you normally buy shares in £5000 lots, make sure the economic exposure you are taking on is no larger than this, even though the down payment (with typical 15% margin) might only be £750. The gearing in a derivative like this allows you to gain a larger amount of exposure than your capital would normally permit. But just because you can get that amount of exposure doesn't mean you *have* to take it.

Key concepts

Derivatives like CFDs (and spread betting) give you geared up profits and losses.

You can limit your exposure by simply staking less.

Hedging

Because they are contracts, and don't involve buying and selling specific physical assets, derivatives allow you to speculate on price movements in either direction. You can sell a share as a CFD without owning the underlying, if you believe the price is likely to fall.

You might do this, for example, if you held a share that had risen sharply. Rather than sell it, you could reduce your exposure to the movement in it on a temporary basis by selling a CFD against the holding. In other words, with derivatives like CFDs, speculation isn't the only choice you have.

A *hedge* is a transaction constructed to produce a compensating profit if the value of another holding falls. There's a cost involved, just as there is with an insurance policy. But sometimes it is right to take out insurance.

Many see derivatives as inherently always risky. They can be, but they don't have to be. Anyone with a capped rate mortgage, or who owns a capital protected bond or unit trust, has a product that only exists courtesy of the hedging possibilities offered by the derivatives markets.

Because they allow hedging, I think that derivatives like CFDs merit the attention of serious investors.

> **Key concept**
>
> Used correctly CFDs allow you to insure your investments against unexpected market events, or neutralise their impact.

Indexes

Understanding how stock market indexes work is crucial to evaluating the derivatives that most investors deal in. These include CFDs, as well as futures, options and spread betting. The indexes on which derivatives are based vary. Most commonly they involve *capitalisation-weighted averages* of their constituents (although the Dow Jones is an exception).

What this means is that the bigger the company in terms of its market capitalisation, the bigger the impact a 1% movement in its price will have on the index. Most broad market indices have recently introduced refinements to this system. These deal with index constituents that have major shareholders. In this instance, the weighting is modified to reflect the fact that a portion of the issued shares is unlikely to be freely tradable. By eliminating major stakes and cross-shareholdings, the weightings in the index more closely reflect the realities of trading in shares in the market. The FTSE 100, the S&P500, the CAC40 in France and DAX in Germany have all moved to this so-called 'free float adjusted' basis over the last few years.

How do indexes like this work in practice?

If you want to trade a CFD in a stock market index, it pays to know precisely how the index works.

Take the FTSE 100 ('footsie'). It was launched with a value of 1000 in mid-1984. It was devised mainly for the benefit of futures traders. They needed an index benchmark that was calculated in a consistent way and that could be used as a proxy for the UK equity market.

With the footsie, an independent committee acts as referee, and decides on the periodic changes that need to be made to the index's constituents. The committee meets quarterly, or more frequently if necessary. Its work is to administer the rules for inclusion and exclusion of particular companies, and to decide what happens in the event of takeovers, right issues, new issues and suspensions.

The ideal is for the footsie to contain the largest 100 companies by market capitalisation at any one time. However, because this can change daily as individual share prices change, the committee reviews the list quarterly and adopts a 90/110 rule. Any company whose market capitalisation has risen to the 90th position or above is automatically included. Any that has fallen below 110th place is ejected.

Companies in the index vary hugely in size

At the time of writing (late November 2008) the biggest company in the FTSE 100, BP, had a market value of eight times the size of, for example, Barclays, the 20th-ranked company and 40 times that of Rexam, which is two-thirds of the way down the top 100 list. This makes a difference to index movements. A 5% price change in BP's market capitalisation of £87 billion would have around 120 times the impact on the index of a similar percentage change in the index's smallest constituent.

The top five companies account for 37% of the index's total value, and the top 10 account for just over half the total.

It's not necessarily a bad thing. Other indices have their quirks as well. But before you deal in a derivative based around a stock market index, make sure you understand exactly the basis on which it's calculated.

Table 2.2: Key features of stock market indices

Index	Country	Constituents	Weighting by:	Free float adj.?
S&P 500	USA	500	Capitalisation	Yes
DJIA	USA	30	Price	No
NASDAQ 100	USA	100	Capitalisation	Yes
FTSE 100	UK	100	Capitalisation	Yes
DAX	Germany	30	Capitalisation	Yes
CAC40	France	40	Capitalisation	Yes
Nikkei	Japan	225	Price	No

Sources: Various

> **Key concept**
>
> There are many derivatives based around stock market indices, including CFDs. The way the indexes are compiled varies. They are a good way of getting diversified exposure to a market. But you need to understand what makes the index tick before dealing in a CFD based on it.

Margin

The idea of margin is integral to many derivatives. Margin is an upfront payment that you make via your broker to guarantee that you can meet the obligations of the contract. You will be asked to deposit margin when you first buy or sell a CFD (*initial margin*). This fixed amount will be a (usually modest) percentage of the contract's underlying size. If the trade moves the wrong way you will be asked for more money to make up the difference (*variation margin*).

The percentage margin required depends on what the broker calculates to be the likely degree to which the price of the underlying share or index might swing around while the trade is open. This is called volatility.

For example, a CFD in a smaller company share will usually require a much bigger margin percentage than, for example, a large stable company like Vodafone. This is because the price of the smaller company is expected to be more volatile. And margin on a stock index will usually be less than that on any individual company.

Some CFD providers ask for 100% margin in the case of highly volatile companies. A CFD on these terms offers few advantages other than the ability to sell short (see below).

Key concepts

Initial margin is the upfront deposit you make when you buy or sell a futures contract.

Additional *variation margin* will be required if your trade goes the wrong way.

Margin means CFDs have *gearing*. Low percentage margin means high gearing.

A quick word on volatility.

Volatility

Volatility is one of the most important concepts when it comes to trading derivatives. It is particularly important in the case of options. But volatility also governs the margin required in CFD trades. Volatility refers to the degree to which the price of a share or index swings around. It can be measured statistically. It differs from share to share and index to index, and it changes hour-by-hour, day-by-day and week-by-week. You can see this in the way a stock market index or a share goes through periods of stability and then moves erratically for a spell.

The bigger the swings in price, the greater the volatility.

Remember though that volatility is a statistical concept and can be precisely measured from a history of price changes.

VIX

In the US volatility has a special index of its own, known as the *VIX*, which reflects the short-term volatility of the S&P500 index, the broad US market benchmark. The following chart shows the VIX since 2005.

Chart 2.1: Chart of the VIX

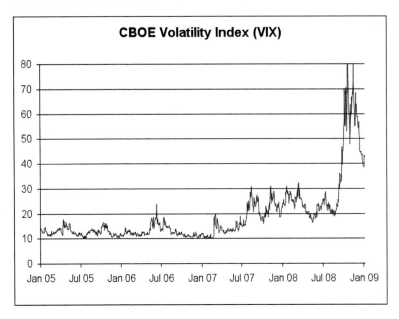

As can be seen, from 2005 to 2006 the VIX fluctuated between 10% and 20%. In 2007 volatility levels increased as the VIX moved between 20% and 30%. Then, in October 2008 at the height of the banking crisis, the VIX (sometimes referred to as the "fear index") soared to 80%.

Because markets worldwide are becoming increasingly correlated, the VIX is closely watched by traders around the world, and its level tends to be broadly reflected in margin rates levied on equity derivatives (such as CFDs). For example, in October 2008 as the VIX hit 80%, margins on some equity CFDs was increased from 10% to – in some cases – 100%.

Key concept

Volatility measures how much the price of an underlying security swings about. It means greater risk for the CFD broker. Margin required on more volatile instruments is higher, to compensate for this risk.

Short Selling

Short selling is a curiosity. It is selling something you don't own in the hope that the price will fall, at which point you buy it back and pocket the difference.

It's a concept that many share investors find difficult to grasp. In the share market, the mechanics of short selling are: borrow the stock from a long-term investor; sell it; buy it back (hopefully at a lower price); and then return it to the lender.

This is complicated, and has always been a professionals' market. Although brokers can borrow stock, they will normally only facilitate short selling for large clients. While it's controversial, it can be argued that it contributes to the smooth running of the market by providing extra liquidity.

But now you don't need the complex mechanics of classic stock market short selling. CFDs allow you to bet on a fall in either an individual stock or the market as a whole.

In other words you can sell short, but without the hassle of borrowing stock.

This is because derivatives are *contracts*. They do not involve the direct buying or selling, or indeed ownership, of the underlying stock or commodity. Therefore you don't have to worry about borrowing or returning stock. There is nothing to stop you selling a share via a CFD without having first bought it. You are simply taking a view that the market in question will fall in the future.

CFDs allow ordinary investors to short sell a wide range of stocks if they wish. Since their introduction to the investment mainstream a few years ago, private investors have had access to the same tools that the professionals have been using for decades. And, obviously, when markets are generally falling, this is important.

Key concept

CFDs allow you a hassle-free way to bet on a *fall* in price instead of a rise.

Comparison With Other Derivatives

The following table compares some features of CFDs and futures, options, spread betting, covered warrants and ETFs.

Question	Futures	Spread Betting	CFDs	ETFs	Options	Covered Warrants
New broker required?	Yes (but can probably use to deal in options)	Yes (but same broker may deal in CFDs)	Yes (but same broker may do spread bets)	No, trade through your existing broker	Yes, but many option brokers trade futures too	Not necessarily
Minimum account size?	Probably	Low	Varies but generally higher than for spread betting	Not applicable	Not necessarily	No
Dealing specifics?	Buy/sell, contract, delivery month	Buy/sell, product, expiry, stake size	Buy/sell, stock/index	Buy/sell, product	Buy or write, stock, put or call, strike, expiry, style	Buy to open, sell to close a specific warrant
Minimum trade size?	£2 per index pt x margin; 1000 x stock price x margin	Yes, but far from onerous	Varies but some have no minimum	No	One contract = 1000 shares or £10 per index point	No, can deal in any size
Margin % needed?	Varies with volatility of underlying. 5-30%	Varies with volatility of underlying – more than futures	Varies but can be less than futures	Not applicable, you have to put up 100%	Not applicable – pay 100% of premium	Not applicable – pay 100% of premium
Spreads?	Tight in index futures, less tight in stock futures	Varies with product and firm – less on dailies	Deal at 'cash' market price	Varies – often possible to deal inside the 'touch'	Varies – often wide on low priced options	Relatively narrow, capped by exchange
Commission?	Varies but usually £10 per lot down to £4	No	Commonly 0.25% of consideration; some charge zero	Yes, as for shares	Yes, often flat rate plus exchange levy	As for shares – often flat rate per trade
Stamp duty?	No	No	No	No	No	No
CGT on gains?	Yes	No	Yes	Yes, as for shares	Yes	Yes

3
How CFDs Work

Some investors regard CFDs, futures and spread betting as roughly similar. It is true that they all work in basically the same way, however there are differences that need taking into account.

Futures and spread betting contracts are essentially the same. Spread betting firms often base contracts around an underlying futures product, although spread bets differ from futures because they are exempt from CGT.

CFDs are subject to CGT but differ from spread bets in positive ways too. One is that the difference between bid and offer prices is almost always substantially less. CFDs on shares are usually available at the price prevailing in the so-called 'cash' market (in this case, this means the normal stock exchange price). CFDs also provide for the payment of an interest credit on a short position.

CFDs, spread bets and futures are not subject to stamp duty. This is because they are paper contracts, one step removed from owning the underlying on which they are based.

At this point, let's review the fundamental things that CFDs do for investors.

1. They are paper contracts.

2. They have a direct link to the price of an underlying investment.

3. They provide gearing, because investors usually only have to put up a modest percentage of the underlying value of the investment by way of margin.

4. They also allow investors, if they wish, a hassle-free way to go short.

But with all derivatives – especially CFDs – *the devil is in the detail*. So let's look at the basics of CFD trading.

CFD Basics

The simplest way of looking at a CFD is to start by thinking of it as a way of buying shares using a short-term loan.

You get a loan to buy the shares, and you pay interest on a daily basis (as you would on any normal loan). When you sell, you use the proceeds to pay off the loan and pocket (or pay) the difference. Because you are borrowing most of the cost of the shares, your return, if the shares go up, is magnified (as with a mortgage on a house). Of course if they go down, your percentage loss is magnified as well.

The table below shows how this works. Assume you buy the Vodafone CFD when the share price is 100, and its price then moves up to 120p or down to 80p. The table shows the result (we'll ignore dealing costs for the purposes of this example):

Example – CFD in 10,000 Vodafone (share price currently 100p)

Vodafone at:	100p	120p	80p
Margin	£2000	£2000	£2000
Underlying value	£10,000	£12,000	£8000
Gain/loss	£0	+£2000	-£2000
Capital after closing trade	£2000	£4000	£0
Return on capital	0%	+100%	- 100%

In other words a 20% move in either direction means the difference between either making a 100% gain on your money or wiping out your starting capital of £2000.

Gearing works both ways

Bear in mind also that you can easily lose more than you put up at the outset. If your initial deposit in the previous example had been 10% rather than 20%, for example, the profits and losses would be the same, but the return on the gain would be 200% and the loss would be double the initial margin deposit. This is the impact of trading with borrowed money.

In short, the smaller the percentage you put up as your initial deposit, by definition the bigger the gearing you have to movements in the underlying share in either direction, and the bigger the potential gains *and losses*.

For example, if margin is 50% then your profit (or loss) will change twice as much as the movement in the underlying – if the underlying increases 20% your position will increase 40%. Now, if margin is 20%, then you will have 5 times gearing: movements in your profit/loss will be 5 times greater than those of the underlying. And if margin is 10%, then you will have gearing of 10 times.

Markets can move extremely rapidly, as can the price of individual shares – even those of the largest, most seemingly stable companies. In late-October 2008, telecoms giant BT issued a profit warning. The shares dropped 20% in a single trading session. That's bad enough if you had owned the shares. A holder of 10,000 BT shares would have lost £2700 on that day. But if you were long a CFD in 10,000 BT shares on, say 15% margin, you would have lost 130% of your initial capital in a single day.

Strict definition of CFDs

We can't, however, simply look at CFDs as akin to buying shares with borrowed money. In the first place, you can use a CFD not just to buy shares but also to go short. Secondly, you never technically own the underlying shares on which a CFD is based.

The more complicated but accurate definition is that a CFD is:

A contract between a buyer and seller to pay, in cash, when the contract is terminated, the difference between the opening and closing value of the shares (or index) on which the contract is based.

In fact the absolutely correct definition is that a CFD is:

a total return equity swap, designed to replicate the economic performance and cash flows of a conventional share investment.

Differences versus futures and spread betting

The mention of cash flows does however hint at some of the differences between CFDs on the one hand, and futures and spread betting on the other.

Open ended

One fundamental difference is that, in the case of a CFD, the contract is normally *open-ended*. There is no expiry date as there is with a future or a futures-based spread bet.

Financing cost

The second difference is that the *cost of the financing* in the contract is separate from the dealing price, not included in it. In a future, for example, the price you pay includes an element that reflects the interest saving you get by buying the future on margin rather than paying for the underlying in full at the outset. This difference narrows as the future approaches the delivery date.

With a CFD, the price you pay is at or very close to the price in the normal cash market, but the interest on the margin loan is debited or credited to your account on a daily basis depending on whether you are going long or short.

Interest is calculated on the terms specified by your CFD provider, but normally debited at a premium to the overnight rate and credited at a discount to the overnight rate. We'll look at this in more detail in a later chapter, but suffice to say that CFD brokers make considerable amounts of money from these premiums and discounts, and also that terms differ between brokers.

Ownership

Although you don't technically own the underlying shares, the contract (and the outside world) assumes you do. This *de facto ownership property* of CFDs is not without controversy. Predators have built stakes in companies through the CFD market, a factor which the targets of their attentions do not view particularly kindly, as the activity is harder to trace.

In fact the Takeover Panel recently amended its rules so that major market players who build a stake in a company using CFDs are subjected to the same rules and restrictions they would have been obliged to follow had they owned their stake entirely in shares.

Dividends

Another idiosyncrasy of CFDs relates to dividends. If you are long (i.e. have bought expecting the price to rise) and the share goes ex-dividend during the time your CFD is open, your account is credited with the net dividend. By the same token if you are short and the same thing happens, your account is debited with the gross dividend.

This contrasts with spread betting and futures. Here there is no right to any dividends on the shares that might be the subject of a bet or a futures trade, although ex-dividend effects tend to be built into futures prices automatically by the market.

Commissions and tax

Finally, CFD brokers in the main do charge commission, usually on the underlying value of the contract. Commission is paid on both the opening and closing sides of a deal, and can be a significant factor in the cost of a trade. We will explore the question of commissions in more detail in the next chapter. But it is worth noting that, as with interest debits and credits, firms differ substantially in the charges they levy.

A commission rate of 0.2% or 0.25% of consideration for each trade is fairly typical, but some firms charge a flat fee per trade. Some firms offer commission-free dealing, but you must assume that they will make it up in other ways, perhaps from more expensive interest debits and meaner credits. **Interactive Investor charges only 0.15% for UK Equity trades and NO commission on Index, Forex or Commodity trades**.

CFDs are exempt from the stamp duty that share transactions attract. They do, however, fall under the CGT regime. Once again this is slightly different from spread betting and futures. Futures get caught by the CGT net, but spread betting doesn't. There is no stamp duty to pay for futures, spread bets, or CFDs, because they are paper contracts rather than physical transactions.

Below is a summary of these basic characteristics.

Basic CFD characteristics

- you can go **long or short**

- **daily interest** is charged (or credited) to your account

- **dividends** are credited (or charged) to your account

- **cash flows** on trades are calculated each day

- you usually deal at the **cash market price**

- **commission** is payable, usually calculated on the underlying contract value

- you are liable to **CGT**, but not to **stamp duty**

The next section looks in more detail at precisely how CFDs work on a day-to-day basis using a worked example. We'll then go on to look at some of the advantages and pitfalls involved in trading CFDs and the rules of the road when it comes to trading them.

CFD Mathematics

Accounting for a CFD trade is a bit more complicated than it is for buying and selling shares.

With shares, the costs are stamp duty at 0.5% of the consideration, and commission, which might be just, say, a flat £14.99 for the buying and selling side. You receive any dividends net.

With CFDs there are more things to consider. Commission (let's assume) is normally charged as 0.25% of *the underlying value of the contract*, and interest is charged or credited depending on whether you are long or short. The dividend is received net or debited gross depending on whether you are long or short. There is no stamp duty.

For both shares and CFDs there is the bid-offer spread to consider.

Let's have a look at how it works in practice.

Example – Comparison of shares and CFDs when going LONG

First of all we need to make some assumptions.

- Commission is £14.99 per trade for shares; 0.25% of consideration for CFD

- Interest is charged on the CFD position at 5.475% (or £1.50 per day for a position of £10,000)

Your objective is to get exposure to £10,000-worth of Vodafone shares.

- The price of Vodafone is now 100p; your CFD margin deposit is 20%

- After three months Vodafone is 110p

- A dividend of 1p is paid just before you close the trade

The table below shows how the P&L account stacks up between shares and the CFD.

Table 3.1: Using CFDs or shares to go long 10,000 Vodafone

	Shares	CFD
Investment at 100p	£10,000	£2000
Underlying holding (shares)	10,000	10,000
Starting value	£10,000	£10,000
Commission	-£14.99	-£25.00
Stamp	-£50.00	Nil
Dividend	£100.00	£100.00
Interest (90 days)	Nil	-£135.00
Sale proceeds at 110p	£11,000	£11,000
Sale commission	-£14.99	-£27.50
Profit incl. dividend	£1100	£1100
Net costs	-£79.98	-£187.50
Net profit	£1020.02	£912.50
Return on capital	10.20%	45.63%

We need to analyse this a bit more closely.

For the same percentage movement in the underlying share price, we have achieved a broadly similar money return, but a much bigger percentage return on the capital we have invested via the CFD. In the CFD we have had the same level of exposure to the underlying shares, but only tied up a fifth of the capital. We have paid interest for the privilege, but we might also have earned interest on the capital we had saved. I haven't counted this in the example.

The net dividend of 1p a share is credited to the CFD as having been received when the shares go ex-dividend (not when the payment to shareholders is made). Commission rates are higher on the CFD than they would be for an execution-only share broker. Total costs for the CFD trade (commission and interest) are substantially higher than the commission and stamp paid on the share transaction.

Now let's look at the same calculation if you are going short.

Example – Comparison of shares and CFDs when going SHORT

This time I'm going to assume that:

- the shareholder already has £10,000-worth of Vodafone shares,

- the CFD trader shorts them at 100p,

- Vodafone shares then go down to 90p, and

- dividend payments, interest, commission and the like are all the same as in the previous example.

There is a slight wrinkle as far as the dividend payment is concerned. When you short a share using a CFD the gross amount of any dividend that occurs during the period is charged to your trade as a cost. This contrasts with the 'long' example above, where the net dividend only is credited. As I've already mentioned, in both cases the credit or charge happens when the shares go ex-dividend, not when the dividend is actually paid.

Many investors are tuned in to the distinction between ex-dividend dates and dividend payment dates. You shouldn't be trading CFDs if you are not aware of this difference.

But just to be clear, the ex-dividend date is the date on and after which a purchaser of the shares is no longer entitled to receive a recently announced dividend payment. On this date, the share price usually adjusts downwards by the amount of the net dividend. Dividend payment dates and ex-dividend dates can sometimes be many weeks, even months, apart. They are known in advance and are invariably disclosed at the time of a results announcement. They sometimes create opportunities for nimble CFD traders.

The profit and loss calculation on the short CFD trade is shown in the following table, and compared with the costs of selling an existing holding of the shares, and then buying them back at the lower price.

Table 3.2: Using CFDs to go short

	Shares	CFD
Capital involved	£10,000	£2000
Underlying holding (shares)	10,000	10,000
Sale value	£10,000	£10,000
Sale Commission	-£14.99	-£25.00
Stamp (on buyback)	-£45.00	Nil
Dividend	0	-£111.00
Interest (90 days)	Nil	+£135.00
Buyback cost	£9000	£9000
Commission on buyback	-£14.99	-£22.50
Loss avoided or profit made	£1000	£1000
Net costs	-£74.98	-£23.50
Net profit	£925.02	£976.50
Return on capital	9.25%	48.83%

Here you can see how to some degree the trade mirrors what happened in the earlier example.

Interest is credited to the CFD rather than debited, but the grossed-up dividend (100 x 0.9) is debited from the CFD account rather than credited. The shareholder does not receive the dividend because (until he buys back the holding) he does not own the shares.

In this instance, the costs of the CFD trade are slightly less than the sale and subsequent buyback of the shares. In fact, though, you do need to account for the fact that the share seller could also earn interest on the £10,000 released by the sale, assuming the CFD broker pays interest on unused balances (some don't).

The return on the capital involved is again much higher in the case of the CFD. In reality the numbers could be even greater than this. Some brokers require only 10% initial margin at present on a Vodafone CFD, although this could change if the shares suddenly become more volatile. Lower margin magnifies the return if you get the trade right, but also magnifies the risk to your capital if you get it wrong.

7 CFD Rules of the Road

There is a temptation to see CFDs as spread betting on steroids. Or maybe spread betting is like CFDs on valium!

Either way, the point is that CFDs generally dictate a much bigger financial commitment and therefore a bigger risk for an investor. Investors using CFDs really do need to be comfortable that the money committed to CFD trading is money they can afford to lose.

This brings us to the number one rule when it comes to trading in CFDs.

Rule #1 – Make sure you can afford it

It sounds obvious, but *you have to be able to afford it*. CFD firms will only open an account for you if they are satisfied that you are an experienced and reasonably affluent investor. This is as much for the protection of their good name as for any interest in your financial well-being. You need to demonstrate that you have been actively trading shares or futures for a long time, or have experience in the investment business, and that you have substantial surplus net assets in a readily liquid form.

The way CFD firms deal with this in practical terms is by setting fairly high minimum amounts that you will be required to deposit in your account before you can begin trading. We'll go into this in more detail in our chapter on dealing, but you will need anything from £5000 to £25,000 as a minimum amount to deposit and further cash in reserve to meet possible margin calls if trades go awry.

Rule #2 – Remember that margin requirements vary from stock to stock

Remember that *margin requirements differ from stock to stock, from instrument to instrument and from broker to broker*. They vary with the underlying volatility of the share, bond or commodity in question. In the case of equities, unless the stock concerned is particularly illiquid, a good rule of thumb is that you can usually borrow between five and ten times the amount of underlying cash deposited. Or, to put it more accurately, if you want to deal in a stock to the tune of an underlying value of £10,000, you probably need to have at least £2000 in your account. You need commensurately more if the stock in question is a smaller company, or if it has a volatile price history. Margin rates on currencies and some commodities – like gold and oil – are typically lower. While margin rates change typical margin rates on the latter can be as little as 2% or even less at some brokers.

The table shows examples of the upfront deposit (or margin) that you need to put up for different types of shares.

Extra margin will be debited from your account or called from you if the trade goes the wrong way.

Table 3.3: Typical initial margin requirements in CFDs

Instrument	Deposit required (% of underlying value)
Stock indices	5% or 10%
UK top 350 (SETS) shares	10% or 20%
UK top 350 (non-SETS) shares	15% or 25%
Other UK shares	25% plus
European shares	10% plus
US shares	10% plus
Options	100% of option premium

Source: CFD brokers

Rule #3 – Use CFDs mainly in shares and stock indexes

At the outset, CFDs were only available on a restricted number of shares and other instruments. The same choice of instruments as you would find with futures and spread betting. This is no longer the case. Although CFDs can in theory be used for trading any stock, stock index, exchange rate or commodity with a liquid underlying price, it is probably still fair to say that they are primarily used for trading shares and stock market indexes. They are to some degree a half-way house between futures and spread betting, bearing in mind the technical differences that we have already mentioned.

With futures you can only trade a limited range of international shares, but you can trade many other instruments and commodities too, including interest rate and bond futures. With CFDs, many brokers confine themselves to trading UK shares and indices, leading foreign shares and indices, and foreign exchange. This is enough for most investors. But most CFD brokers will provide a CFD product in almost anything if customers request it. Many CFD brokers offer trading in CFDs on bullion and soft commodities.

Rule #4 – Integrate CFD trading with the rest of your investing

If you want to trade CFDs, make sure that it forms an *integrated part of your overall investing activity*. Reputable firms that offer CFDs and spread betting – and many do both – frequently say they want their clients to make dealing in them only a part of their overall trading. It should be complementary to, rather than competing with, your conventional share buying and selling.

One reason for this is that CFD buyers will rarely make money through doing single speculative transactions one after the other. The cannier traders tend to use CFDs in conjunction with an underlying holding or portfolio, in other words as a hedge, or else use combinations of CFDs simultaneously that spread and even neutralise some of the risk that they are running.

We'll cover this later in the chapter on strategies, but a good example might be what is known as *pairs trading*. You might think Vodafone is cheap relative to BT. By shorting a CFD of BT and going long a similar underlying amount in a CFD of Vodafone, you are giving effect to this view. At the same time, you reduce the risk that you will be hurt by a general downturn in the market as a whole or the telecoms sector in particular.

Rule #5 – Monitor your trades closely, especially gearing

Trading in CFDs gives you the ability to assume huge amounts of gearing and a commensurate amount of risk. Many large shares can be traded with as little as 10% margin. This means you magnify the effect of a change in the price of the shares tenfold in terms of its effect on your wallet. Put another way, your capital will be hit very badly indeed if the price moves sharply against you.

In October and November 2008, share prices and indices moved in ways not seen by investors for a generation or more. Some put the October 2008 banking crisis as the worst since the early 1930s. The full details have yet to emerge but, as was the case with private options traders in 1987, the chances are that some private investors have made ruinous losses in CFDs during the course of the crisis.

Even in normal market conditions CFDs need strong nerves, constant monitoring, iron risk control, and a lot of money even before you start playing. Risk control is a separate subject in itself.

Rule #6 – Remember that stop-losses may not be available in all cases

Because of the gearing you have at your disposal in a CFD, if you want to limit your risk you may be able to do so via controlled risk protection, known as a *guaranteed stop-loss*. One point that it's vital to remember here is that stop-losses may not be available on *all* CFD transactions, so you need to check before you deal. Brokers are not stupid, and they will not want to have guaranteed stops in either very volatile or very illiquid shares. Stop-losses are also generally not available in CFDs on options, whereas you may be able to have them when you deal in options through a conventional options broker.

Because there is no time limit on a CFD trade in a normal share, you might feel that having a stop-loss is less important than it would be in a futures trade or spread bet. This is not true. The speed with which an individual share can move the wrong way and blow a hole in your account sometimes startles newcomers to the market. Unless there is a natural hedge for your CFD – like a holding of the underlying shares or a countervailing position in another CFD (as in the pairs trade example above), *you should seriously consider only trading where you can have a guaranteed stop-loss in place.* Stop-losses cost extra but they are well worth the extra cost for peace of mind.

Rule #7 – Keep track of commission and interest costs

As the previous example shows, once the different costs are taken into account, a similar capital commitment to a stock – long or short – made via a CFD rather than an underlying share purchase, will, as a rough rule of thumb, produce a little under five times the return on capital if the investment moves in the right direction. This is on the assumption that you have to put up 20% of the underlying value as an initial margin deposit. If the deposit percentage is lower, say 10%, the gearing will be commensurately higher, around nine times after costs.

Commission charges are typically higher on a CFD than on an underlying share transaction if you buy and sell shares using an execution only broker and deal in reasonable size. This is because CFD commission is based on the total underlying value of the shares you are trading, not the amount you put down in initial margin or the size of the margin loan. Some CFD brokers offer commission-free trading on some instruments, but here the cost of the commission charge is either built into the spread or, more likely, into the interest charge on the margin loan.

There is no such thing as a free lunch.

It also follows that in deciding when and what shares to go short or long of, you should monitor ex-dividend dates and the amount of the dividend paid on that particular date very closely indeed, since these will be debited or credited to your account.

Summary of the 7 CFD Rules of the Road

1. Make sure you can afford it

2. Remember that margin requirements vary from stock to stock

3. Use CFDs mainly in shares and stock indexes

4. Integrate CFD trading with the rest of your investing

5. Monitor your trades closely, especially gearing

6. Remember that stop-losses may not be available in all cases

7. Keep track of commission and interest costs

A Final Word on Gearing and Risk

Gearing is a double edged tool. It's obvious that it works both ways – *for* you if things go right, and *against* you if they don't.

Control your gearing

But it pays to look at gearing another way. If you are accustomed to dealing in shares in, let's say, £10,000 lumps, then if you substitute a CFD trade for a share trade, all it needs to mean is that you tie up less capital. You can get £10,000 of exposure for £2000 and use the remaining £8000 to earn risk-free interest or invest elsewhere. You should not feel compelled to trade in amounts that are five or ten times the level you would normally deal in, simply because CFDs allow you to do so. This is a lesson that many investors learn the hard way.

Some private investors like the idea that they are dealing in tens of thousands of pounds-worth of shares, but those that do this often don't appreciate the risks they are running – until it is too late. While one or two trades like this might be lucky and make substantial profits, trading beyond your means just because you can is usually a recipe for disaster.

Greater diversification

The other side of the coin is that the economical use of capital that CFDs provide can allow you to diversify more easily with the resources at your disposal. One use of gearing is that CFDs would, say, allow you to get exposure to five different shares worth £50,000 in total, for the same £10,000 you might commit to one share via a share purchase. We'll show how this works in a subsequent chapter on trading strategies. Provided the shares are not correlated, this route could be a better, more diversified and less risky way of proceeding than simply putting £10,000 into buying one share that may promptly suffer a profit warning.

It is not a foolproof approach. Investments in shares that may seem uncorrelated may nonetheless all go down together in a major market setback. But financial theory suggests that as few as five truly disparate shares can offer almost the same effective diversification as buying into an index fund. And, of course, with CFDs you are not simply confined to investing in shares. You can easily buy CFDs in bonds and interest rates, bullion, and other completely different asset classes to shares. We'll see how this works in the chapter on strategies.

Minimum account and trade sizes

There are a number of differences between CFD brokers, and you need to be aware of them before you start out trading and, in fact, before you even get around to opening an account.

Above all, make sure the broker fits in with what you want to do, not the other way round. What you do need to bear in mind, for example, is that not only do CFD brokers have minimum deposit levels for opening an account (typically £2000 to £5000), but some also stipulate minimum trade sizes. You may not be able to open a CFD trade unless, for instance, you are prepared to deal in a contract with an underlying value of at least £10,000.

Brokers differ in the interest they pay on unused cash balances in your account, and on whether these funds are segregated from the other assets and liabilities of the firms in question. In view of the recent crisis of confidence in the banking sector, you need to be clear on what might happen to your spare funds in the event of the broker becoming insolvent.

So when you are choosing a broker with which to deal, pay particular attention not only to minimum *balance size* but also to minimum *trade sizes* too. If you can't find a broker that will allow you to open an account and deal in sizes that are comfortable to you, then it's best to look elsewhere.

4
Dealing

Even if you are experienced at dealing in shares and bonds, you really need to read this chapter if you are planning a foray into the world of CFDs.

It looks first at the specifics of placing orders in CFDs. It also looks at the costs involved – some of these may be hidden from view, so you need to take care. The next chapter covers some of the strategies you can employ. Again, you need to examine all of the cost angles before you trade. It's not particularly time-consuming or complicated, but it may save you money.

Let's take a look at some of the angles.

Ten questions to ask yourself about dealing

1. Do you need a new broker to trade CFDs?

2. Do you have to deposit a minimum amount to open an account with the broker?

3. What do you need to specify when dealing?

4. What's the lowest financial commitment per trade?

5. What are its margin requirements?

6. How big is the bid-offer spread?

7. What is the commission for the size of order you want to make?

8. Is commission a flat rate or percentage?

9. What size of position should you take?

10. Should you use a stop-loss order?

We can answer some of these questions easily. But remember the differences, particularly between CFDs and spread betting. CFDs have tight spreads, and are free of stamp duty, but bear CGT. Spreads on spread betting are wider, but gains are free of CGT. CFDs, like futures and spread betting, involve margin payments. The percentage margin differs between and with products. CFD commission is normally a percentage of the underlying consideration. This contrasts with futures, which often have commission charged at a flat rate per contract.

Some CFD brokers also have a spread betting arm, but the chances are you will not be able to switch between the two products in the same account.

CFDs have no time limit involved, whereas futures, almost all spread bets, and options and covered warrants do. CFDs and spread bets can be done on a wide variety of stocks and other instruments. Guaranteed stop-losses are usually available for CFDs.

Remember also the central point about CFD trading: long-only or short-only positions in CFDs (and of course in spread bets and futures) involve gearing in both directions and no limit to profits and losses, unless of course you employ a stop-loss. Even here, however, risk of loss is not completely eliminated.

It all goes to show that the detail is important.

With that in mind, since you may need to open a new broking account to take full advantage of CFDs, a brief word on account-opening procedures, and the points you need to look for and establish at the outset, follows.

Opening an Account

Application form

These days there is none of the mumbo jumbo there used to be about getting an introduction to a broker. Brokers will deal with anyone, provided the new client meets certain financial criteria.

The broker's application form will ask for the usual personal information, your bank details and also some financial details including your income, and the value of your savings and investments, as well as the equity you own in your own home. This gives the CFD broking firm an idea of your financial worth. It wants to know how good a credit risk you are and how large an account to permit you to have.

The broker also needs to know whether or not you are an experienced investor. Regulations stipulate that products like CFDs are only for experienced investors. A relevant point might be, for example, whether or not you are graduating to CFDs from, say, spread betting. This latter point is important, because it shows that you have had some experience of leveraged investments and how quickly they can lose money, and that you know how margin accounts operate.

Credit worthiness of the client

Questions about the size of your investment portfolio and other assets you may have are there for one reason only: so that the broker can be sure that if you lose heavily, you are not at risk of defaulting on your obligations. CFD providers rarely spell it out, but they look for an individual to have investable assets (this does not include your home or any other illiquid investments) in the region of £250,000 to £500,000. Your investment portfolio can be pledged as collateral to satisfy minimum account size and margin requirements.

The firm may also wish to know if you have accounts open with other brokers, and (as I've already indicated) how experienced or otherwise you are at stock market trading in general. Brokers need to make sure that anyone dealing in products like this is fully conversant with the risks involved.

You will have to provide evidence of your assets and also proof of identity and proof of address. This is designed to thwart would-be money-launderers. You may need to provide proof that you have a certain amount of freely available cash. A good rule of thumb is an absolute minimum of liquid funds roughly double the account size you are requesting. Some brokers will also ask for proof of extra liquidity if you are self-employed or your earnings are irregular.

Day-to-Day Trading

CFD trading is slightly different to trading futures or spread betting. All three products do, however, share the same basic characteristics of trading on margin and the possibility of unlimited profits or losses.

What's the difference between trading CFDs, trading futures and spread betting?

With CFDs, the contract is simply between you and the CFD broker. It is not tied to a specific futures product in the way a spread bet may be. Nor is it traded through an exchange the way a future is. The CFD firm may lay off its exposure in the futures market to some degree, but that is a different matter.

It follows from this that CFD brokers can be much more creative in how they operate their business. With some brokers you can, for example, deal through the night if you so wish. Trading is not confined to prescribed market hours. **The Interactive Investor platform is available for trading 24 hours a day with 24 hour telephone trading.**

Before we look at this in more detail let's home in on our earlier list of key questions, by looking at the following table.

Table 4.1: CFD dealing specifics

Question	Answer
New Broker?	Yes (but same broker may do spread bets)
Min. account size?	Varies but generally higher than for spread betting
Dealing specifics?	Buy/sell, stock/index/other instruments
Minimum trade size?	Varies but some have no minimum
Margin % needed?	Varies but can be less than futures
Spreads?	Deal at cash market price
Commission?	Commonly 0.2% or 0.25% of consideration
Stamp duty?	No
CGT on gains?	Yes
Stop-losses available?	Yes

Commission

Interactive Investor has competitive commission rates on all Equity Trading, with NO commission on Index, Forex or Commodity trades.

Interest debits and credits

It's important to check the exact details of how much interest is charged for long positions – or credited on short positions. The details change with different brokers, who can use any formulation they like.

In practice, financing costs are usually calculated relative to either:

- LIBOR (London Inter Bank Offered Rate), or
- the Bank of England's Base Rate.

LIBOR is the most common reference, but some brokers use the Base Rate. In normal times, LIBOR tracks the Base Rate fairly closely, but in 2007 the two rates diverged quite markedly (which led to one or two problems that we won't go into here).

CFD financing charges will usually be quoted something like "LIBOR +/- 2%", which means that:

- **long positions** will be *charged* at a rate of LIBOR +2%, and
- **short positions** will be *credited* at a rate of LIBOR -2%

So, for example, if sterling 3-month LIBOR is currently 2.06% (which it is at the time of writing), then a broker using a formulation "LIBOR +/- 2%" would charge 4.06% on long positions, and credit 0.06% on short positions. In practice, the rates used by brokers range from +/-1.25% to +/-3.00% and are charged/credited on a daily basis.

The values for interest charges may seem small to an equity investor, but over time the charges (for a long position) mount up. For example, if an investor has an open long CFD position of value £20,000, and his broker charges LIBOR +3% (when LIBOR is 2.06%), then the investor's account will be debited £2.77 every day. That may not seem much, but over six months the financing charge would amount to £526. That's 2.63% of the position value – more than all the transaction costs combined.

In fact, beyond a certain point, the costs of a holding a position in an equity CFD are greater than holding the underlying shares.

Which is why CFDs are suitable for short-term trading, but not for long-term investing.

This rather runs counter to what is sometimes touted as the big difference between CFDs on the one hand, and futures related products on the other: there are no time limits on CFDs, whereas with futures you need to pay attention to delivery dates. While that's true, the interest element has to be factored in and interest costs on a long position can mount up.

Margin

Initial margin may be somewhat lower on a CFD than on a stock future. In the past, for example, Some brokers have quoted 3% initial margin on Vodafone (although this isn't a particularly volatile share these days, so may not be a particularly good benchmark). Many brokers levy margin at around 10% on most equity CFDs, but only around 5% on index CFDs.

Having said that, it is difficult to generalise.

The margin requirement is essentially based around the volatility of the instrument in question. Sucden, for example, quotes the following broad parameters, and many other brokers would arguably concur:

Table 4.2: Margin rates

Market	Margin
Indices	5%
Low risk stocks	10%
Medium risk stocks	15%
High risk stocks	25%
Very high risk stocks	50%
Extreme risk stocks	100%

This is broadly consistent with the rates quoted in the table earlier. But it does show that it is impossible to generalise when it comes to determining what sort of margin you might pay. Outside of the stock market, margin on currency trades is typically around 2% of the underlying contract value in gold and silver 5%, and in bonds 1.5%.

Tick value

It's important to understand the relationship between the so-called 'tick' value and margin requirements. The *tick* is the minimum movement in the underlying price and a tick movement usually equates to a one unit movement in the underlying currency. In other words a movement from, say, 9549 to 9450 in a short sterling (i.e. short-term UK interest rate) CFD would change the unit value of a CFD position by £1.

Tick sizes vary from instrument to instrument and this aspect of trading needs to be thoroughly understood before you commit money to the market. Deal spreads vary considerably from instrument to instrument and may be quoted by a broker in, for example, a brochure or terms and conditions document, either in absolute terms or relative to the underlying spread in the market.

One factor to bear in mind is that spreads can widen near the open and close of trading, can be significantly larger outside of normal market hours, and widen if market conditions are particularly volatile.

CFD firms do, however, operate in a highly competitive market. So the spreads quoted by CFD market makers are likely to be highly competitive in most areas of the market, differing only in those areas to which a particular firm might not wish to be exposed.

Stop-loss orders

As with spread betting, guaranteed 'stop-loss' orders are available in CFDs as are a variety of other types, including trailing stop-loss orders.

A normal stop-loss order (something that many CFD brokers call a 'guaranteed stop-loss') is an order that automatically closes an open trade if the price moves adversely beyond a pre-set level. Stop-loss orders are often set to establish a 'pain barrier' beyond which any losses will be cut. In absolute terms too, they are often placed at key chart support and resistance levels which, if the price were to break through, might be the precursor to a sharp further movement in the same direction. [We'll see how these work in a later chapter.].

Trailing stop-losses

To recap, a stop-loss order can be set to trigger at a fixed absolute price level. But in the case of trailing stop-losses, it can also be set to trigger (in normal circumstances) if a security falls by a specified percentage below its previous recent high, set during the period since the trade has been open. In other words it would, in an ideal world, lock in an increasing amount of profits following a steady rise, but trigger if a previous uptrend starts to falter.

Guaranteed stop-losses

CFD brokers call stop-losses 'guaranteed' because they do not need to be put through the underlying 'cash' market to be executed. This is because the CFD is a contract between the client and the broker. If the contract stipulates closing the trade at a specific price, then that is what should happen. This contrasts with a stop-loss order in a normal share where, even if a broker can be found who will agree to take such an order, the order has to be executed in the market for it to have any effect.

With CFDs this is not the case. And a range of other conditions can be set that will come into force automatically. Clients can stipulate, for example, that if they close a trade, a previously set stop-loss is automatically cancelled.

Traders should, however, be aware that the guarantee in a guaranteed stop-loss is sometimes not all it would seem. Contract or no, the market has to be open and operating normally for a guaranteed stop-loss to be executed.

If there is a sharp downward adjustment to the market, or in the price of a share, as a result of an event announced over a weekend (let's say, a terrorist incident, or a company in which you have a long CFD going bust), then the price will gap down at the opening next day and the guaranteed stop-loss will be unable to be executed at the price you previously chose.

The CFD broker will, in these instances, claim *force majeure* and invoke the inevitable small print get-out clause in the contract. In other words, though guaranteed stop-losses are essential for trading CFDs, you need to be keenly aware that circumstances can arise where the guarantee will be invalid.

The bottom line is that what you have at risk in a CFD – in the absolute worst case scenario – is liability for the full underlying amount of the contract. This is particularly true for a CFD on an individual share. A company can go bust and its shares become worthless overnight. In practice what happens is that, in cases of extreme market movements, the stop-loss order is executed at the best available price.

There are illustrations of the way stop-loss orders work in mathematical terms in the next chapter. You pay extra for stop-losses. Brokers vary in their terms but a typical charge might be, for example, 0.3% of the consideration when opening the trade. Another way of looking at this is that commission is substantially higher for a trade with a stop-loss order built in.

Account opening requirements

Account opening requirements for CFDs are somewhat similar to spread betting in terms of the procedures that need to be completed. There are forms to fill and evidence of identity and proof of address to be provided.

But remember that CFD firms generally demand a higher minimum deposit and want clients that are both experienced and reasonably well-heeled financially. Some CFD firms want clients with accounts of a minimum £20,000, although some will accept able or willing to commit £5000, or even as little as £2000.

Brokers are duty bound to investigate thoroughly the financial position of prospective clients, and a member of the trading team is likely to discuss this with a would-be new account holder before trading is permitted.

Although the minimum deposit requirements are relatively low, realistically speaking the more cash in your account the better and it is likely that, if you only have £2000 or £5000 to spare to put into a CFD account, then trading CFDs (or indeed any leveraged product) is not really suitable. A few brokers offer advisory services, but the more normal execution-only model of doing business tends to apply.

Interest on unused balances

Most CFD brokers pay interest on unused balances – although in these days of ultra-low interest rates, not much. This is separate and distinct from the financing paid and received as a result of long or short CFD positions. Before deciding how much to commit to a CFD account it is as well to check not only the standing of the broker concerned, but also the interest paid on idle cash balances. Most brokers should pay a rate similar to the credit interest on short positions.

A more contentious point is to determine precisely how safe these balances are. Do they, for example, represent an underlying account at a well known and reputable third party bank or does the account simply rest on the creditworthiness of the CFD broker? Are cash balances fully segregated from the broker's own assets and liabilities and placed in a client account?

Brokers' terms and conditions change and some brokers appear to be moving towards a position where client balances are not segregated and therefore potentially at risk if the firm were itself to encounter financial difficulties. This point should be thoroughly checked before you commit to one broker in favour of another.

Dealing procedures

Dealing procedures for CFDs are different from, for example, spread bets. With CFDs, punters deal in numbers of shares, so you might for example put on a 'buy-to-open' CFD in 5000 Vodafone shares, asking the price in the normal way and dealing almost as you would in the underlying shares. The terminology would run something like this:

'Buy to open 5000 Vodafone as a CFD at best.'

In reality you would probably ask for the price 'as a CFD' before you dealt. Some CFD brokers also deal in shares too, so it is important to make this distinction during any conversation with a dealer.

'Buy to open' indicates that you are going 'long' and not buying to 'close' an earlier short sale. If dealing by phone, do not indicate whether you are a buyer or a seller before you ask the price.

The only real difference between buying a share and buying a CFD comes in the margin and gearing element, and in the fact that interest is charged on a long position and credited on a short one.

As we will see in a later section, many brokers offer internet-based screen dealing systems for CFD clients, which allow for the opening and closing of trades without any direct contact with a voice broker. These are generally a much easier way to proceed with an execution-only account. Only if you require an advisory service will it be necessary to speak to a broker before placing an order.

5
Trading Strategies

This section deals with trading strategies for CFDs. You will learn how you can use the strategies to boost your returns and reduce your risk.

Many strategies for trading CFDs are similar to those used for spread bets and futures. This is because the overriding characteristics of all these products are similar. There is gearing to movements in the underlying. This is implicit in the fact that the products are traded on margin.

More than simple speculation

Before starting, there is one general point to stress. You can use these products simply as geared-up directional trades. In other words, you can use them to back your view that a particular market or share will rise (or fall) within a set period of time. In this case you go long (or short) using a CFD.

This is the common way investors think of these products: to use them simply as a means for speculating.

But there is more to it than that.

The more subtle way to use these products is in combination with each other, or with an existing shareholding, to reduce or control the risks you are running.

It boils down to a choice:

1. you can use CFDs to take on higher risk in order to generate a higher return, but

2. you can also use them in different ways to provide risk reduction for a portfolio or in an individual stock.

CFDs can, too, be a way of backing your judgement about the relative value of different shares.

The strategies for CFD trading fall into several different headings. Because this is a book about CFDs, I will use CFD-related examples.

The strategies we can use are:

1. Long only / short only for gearing

2. Using stop-losses

3. Cash extraction

4. Pairs trading

5. Relative value

6. Hedging a stock or portfolio

7. Using CFDs to aid asset allocation

8. Exploiting market anomalies

Over the rest of this chapter we'll look at these eight strategies.

I'll talk about the strategies with reference to CFDs. But, apart from some minor technicalities, what holds good for CFD strategies also holds good for strategies using their close cousins in the futures and spread bet areas.

1. Long-Only or Short-Only Trades

CFDs are ideal if all you want is a cheap way of speculating on a rise or fall in the price in an individual share, index, or commodity.

Let's take the case of shares.

You can simply buy a CFD rather than buy the individual share. A CFD will move, more or less, penny for penny with the underlying share price. The gearing comes from the fact that, as we found out in an earlier chapter, when you buy (or sell) a CFD you only have to pay a relatively small initial deposit (called *margin*) to get your exposure to the underlying value of the contract.

To recap this important point: your CFD broker will tell you how much margin you need to put up. It will differ for each individual stock or each different type of contract. Let's say for the sake of argument that you have deposited £50,000 with a CFD broker and the firm has said that it will allow you to trade CFDs in a range of shares with an underlying value at any one time not exceeding £250,000. In effect this means that the amount you have to pledge from your account each time you trade averages out at 20% of the underlying value of the trades you make.

One way of looking at this is that if you normally deal in shares by buying £10,000-worth of stock for each holding, you can get the same amount of exposure with a fifth of the capital. Or you can get five times the exposure you might normally assume for the same amount of capital.

This is an important point.

CFD trades *can* be used to gear up your exposure, but they *don't have to be* used that way. You can simply buy the same amount of exposure you normally take on, but use a fifth of the capital you would normally, and earn interest on the unused amount. We'll return to this point shortly.

Let's now look at an example.

Example 5.1: Simple CFD position, Vodafone

Initial parameters

- You're confident about the short-term outlook for Vodafone at 100p.

- The CFD price is 100-101.

- You buy 10,000 shares as a CFD.

- This gives you exposure to 10,000 shares in Vodafone.

- The margin required is (say) roughly £2000.

Now, let's say that Vodafone shares rise by 10p.

Result

1. If you'd held the underlying shares you would have had £10,000 of capital tied up, and your holding would now be worth £11,000. You'd have made a return of 10%.

2. Holding the CFD position, however, your profit of £1000 is generated by only £2000 of capital pledged, giving you a return on the investment of 50%. That's to say you make a return on capital five times greater than from holding the underlying shares.

Note: in practice, you need to factor in the bid-offer spread as well, and commission, both of which reduce your return. In a CFD trade the spread should be broadly similar to the one in the underlying shares.

The danger of gearing

Don't forget one of the big lessons of CFD trading: if you are using CFDs simply to gear up your exposure, the gearing works both ways. If you guess wrong, your losses are magnified in exactly the same way as your profits are when your judgement is correct. Extending the example above, a downward move of 10% in Vodafone would wipe out half of the capital you'd committed to the trade. Dealing costs and the spread would increase the pain.

Short selling

It's important to remember that you can speculate on a drop in price as easily as on a rise in price.

You do this by selling short. In the case of a CFD, this simply means that your opening transaction is a sell order 'as a CFD'. You make money if the price subsequently goes down. It doesn't matter that you don't own the stock. This is because the CFD is a financial contract, and does not involve a transaction in the underlying shares. The same margin rules apply whether you are long or short. The gearing element is the same, except of course that in the case of short sale, you lose money if the stock rises.

Key points: long-only/short-only speculation with CFDs

- Buy 'as a CFD' to speculate on price rise in underlying

- Sell (short) 'as a CFD' to speculate on price fall in underlying

- Price moves penny for penny with underlying

- Gearing comes from trading on margin (probably at least 5:1)

- Trade like this only with stop-losses

- Monitor trades constantly

- Know your market

2. Long-Only or Short-Only Trades Using Stop-Losses

You should seriously consider using stop-loss orders to control risk. Stop-losses are placed at the time you execute your initial trade. They are orders that will be executed automatically on your behalf if the price moves the wrong way beyond a certain pre-determined level. They can be used to limit your risk in both a long or short position.

- A stop-loss on a **long** position stops your loss if the underlying price *falls* below a certain level, perhaps because of worse than expected news from the company.

- A stop-loss on a **short** position would stop your loss if the price of the underlying *rises* above a certain level, perhaps because of better than expected news from a company, or a takeover bid.

Here's a simple example of how it works.

Example 5.2: Using a stop-loss

Let's say Vodafone is 150p and you want to short it. You hope it's going to go back down to 110p. But if it goes up to 155p it will break a key chart level and might go much higher. You place your initial order to sell at 150p with a stop-loss order (to buy back and close the trade) if it hits 155p. Your maximum loss would be capped at 5p a share.

Guaranteed stop-losses

Guaranteed stop-losses are available for CFDs. But you will pay extra in the form of a wider spread or extra commission charges.

As we noted in the previous chapter, however, you need to bear in mind with a stop-loss that, if the market or an individual share gaps up or down (i.e. opens substantially above or below the previous closing level) because of an event that occurs while the market is closed, it may not be possible to execute the stop-loss at the specified price.

Second, guaranteed stop-losses cost money, in terms of extra commission paid at the outset whether they are triggered or not. So you pay for the guarantee upfront whether or not it turns out to be needed. The guarantee is not 100% solid, but will be applied if your stop-loss point is triggered in normal day-to-day market conditions.

That's not to say that you shouldn't use stop-losses wherever possible, and particularly on share CFDs. Shares are subject to company-specific influences such as takeover bids, poor results, sudden management changes, adverse company announcements, risk of insolvency and a whole range of other factors. Having a stop-loss in place frees you from the need to stay glued to the screen while your position is open. Leveraged investments can lose money extremely quickly. It pays to have a backstop in place.

How do you choose the right position to place a stop-loss?

Place it too close to the prevailing price and your position might be stopped out due to normal day-to-day market fluctuations. Place it too loosely and you might incur needlessly large losses.

Most traders place stop-loss orders with an eye to two factors. First is the pain barrier in percentage or absolute terms beyond which they do not wish to venture. The second is any significant barriers on the price chart that, if broken, might lead to an accelerated move in the wrong direction. We'll look in greater detail at how this works in a later chapter. In the meantime here is an example of how a stop-loss works.

Example 5.3: Guaranteed stop-loss, Experian

Initial parameters

- You're confident about the short-term outlook for Experian at 363p.
- The CFD price is 363-363.5.
- You buy 2000 shares as a CFD.
- This gives you exposure to 2000 shares in Experian.
- You place a stop-loss at 350p.

Implications

The most you can lose on this position is £270. This is 2000 shares x 13.5 (the difference between your buying price of 363.5p and the stop of 350p).

There are charges. Commission at the 0.2% standard rate would be would be £14.54. A premium of 0.3% for the stop-loss would be charged at the outset. This is a further £21.81, and then a further £14 in commission would be incurred if the order were to be executed. This means charges, excluding daily interest costs on the long position, would be a total of £50.35.

Now let's say that Experian shares fall sharply within a few hours to315p, while you are away from your desk.

Result

You have peace of mind. Your stop-loss was triggered at 350p, making your total loss including charges £320.35.

Had you not had the stop-loss in place and had been unable to sell until the price reached 315p, your loss would have been 48.5p a share, or £970 before charges.

Stop-losses like this are the most common use of this sort of device, but they are not the only variant. The other main type used is a trailing stop-loss.

Trailing stop-loss

A trailing stop-loss is a way of locking in profits, as they occur, if you expect an underlying price to be relatively volatile. In the stock market it is common for stop-losses to be raised on an ad hoc basis so they remain a fixed percentage below the prevailing price, often around 15%.

One market rule is that any growth stock should always be sold if it ever drops more than 15% from a recent all-time high. In CFDs, a more formal rule is needed, in particular to determine the initial distance of the stop-loss point from the current price, and also the amount by which the trailing stop-loss moves in response to changes in the underlying price.

The example below, adapted from an illustration on the IG Market website, shows how a trailing stop-loss might be applied to a CFD trade on the Euro/US dollar exchange rate.

Example 5.4: Trailing stop-loss, EURUSD

Initial parameters

- In the short term you think the Euro will rise against the US dollar.

- The current CFD quote for EURUSD is 1.4702-1.4704.

- You buy 2 contracts as a CFD. Contracts are at $10 per point

- This gives you exposure to $20 of loss or gain per 1 point movement.

- You set a trailing stop distance at 30 points (ticks) and a step size of 10 points (ticks).

Scenario

The trailing stop is initially placed at 1.4674 (30 ticks below the trade entry price). The Euro rises against the dollar, reaching a price of 1.4714. This is 10 ticks above your buying price, so the stop-loss steps up to 1.4684 to re-establish the 30 point distance between the current price and the stop-loss trigger.

The rise continues and in a few hours the stop has been re-set several times, with the price then standing at 1.4769 and the stop-loss is at 1.4736.

A subsequent setback in the price takes the rate back to the original starting point.

The stop-loss is triggered at 1.4736, which leaves you with a 32 tick gain, or a profit of $640, less commission.

Result

This is a much better outcome than a conventional stop-loss. This would have been set below the trade entry of 1.4704 and would therefore not have been triggered. The profit would have to be locked-in manually and you may not have been nimble enough to do this. Using a trailing stop in this way is a common ploy in markets like this. The cost is relatively modest, a few points on each side of the trade.

3. Cash Extraction Trades

We saw in the previous section that it is the fact that CFDs (and futures and spread bets) operate on margin that allows investors in them to gear up their return. But we can turn this idea on its head.

Because you can buy a CFD on, say, 20% margin (sometimes lower with less volatile shares) you can achieve the same exposure to an individual stock with a fifth of the capital. Let's say you have a portfolio of four stocks with £5000 invested in each. Ideally you would want to have more stocks than this to achieve better diversification, and perhaps have some extra cash available in case other opportunities come along. Let's assume all your stocks have CFDs available on them.

Your portfolio looks like this:

Table 5.1: Your share portfolio, before cash extraction

Holding	Company	Current price	Value
1000	Archimedes plc	500p	£5000
2000	Brutus plc	250p	£5000
4000	Cassius plc	125p	£5000
1000	Doric plc	500p	£5000

Now let's do the cash extraction and see what happens. In simple terms you are substituting CFDs for your shareholdings in the same proportions, and the amount you can extract will depend on the margin requirements. *After cash extraction* your portfolio looks like this:

Table 5.2: Your CFD portfolio, after cash extraction

Shares	Company	Price	Value	Margin %	Cash committed
1000	Archimedes	500	£5000	20%	£1000
2000	Brutus	250	£5000	15%	£750
4000	Cassius	125	£5000	25%	£1250
1000	Doric	500	£5000	10%	£500
				Total cash committed	£3500
				Cash extracted to keep in reserve or invest elsewhere	£16,500

This brings up a couple of points. One is that we have ignored dealing costs and interest debits in the example above. The second is to do with the mechanics of margin.

Margin calls

Although you have retained your original economic exposure for a fraction of the capital commitment you had previously, you aren't exactly free to do as you wish with this cash. If any of the stocks go down in price, you will be required to provide additional margin, so you need either to have stop-losses in place to keep the falls to a minimum, or keep plenty of cash in reserve for margin calls. Some of the sharp falls in share prices seen in the major market adjustment in October 2008 were as a result of CFD traders making forced sales of stocks to cover margin calls.

So let's say that you decide to keep some of the cash in reserve, but use the rest to buy an index future and two more CFD contracts. Your portfolio after this operation is now represented by Table 5.3.

Your total investment exposure here is still only £20,000, of which £11,250 is committed and £8750 is held in reserve in case of margin calls. The difference is striking. Instead of having only four stocks held in the cash market, which is arguably insufficient to ensure effective diversification, you have six stocks and the index future, which should be more than enough to give you diversification.

There is a slight flaw here, of course. It is that unless you take great care to have a very diverse range of stocks, all of the investments may go bad at the same time. You need to watch how closely these stocks' prices have been correlated with one another in the past, and how volatile they are likely to be for any given movement in the market. We have, however, used this illustration to show how it is possible for even those with limited amounts of capital to use CFDs to achieve a much more balanced portfolio.

Table 5.3: Your CFD portfolio after reinvestment

Share	Company	Price	Value	Margin %	Cash Committed
1000	Archimedes	500	£5000	20%	£1000
2000	Brutus	250	£5000	15%	£750
4000	Cassius	125	£5000	25%	£1250
1000	Doric	500	£5000	10%	£500
2000	Epsilon	250	£5000	20%	£1000
1000	Fourier	500	£5000	15%	£750
1	FTSE future	4000	£40,000	15%	£6000
				Total cash committed	£11,250
				Cash in reserve	£8750

Here's a summary of what we can learn from this.

Cash extraction – key points

- Use cash extraction to economise on capital.

- Use cash extraction to increase diversification.

- Keep cash in reserve for margin calls.

- Use stop-losses on trades to avoid heavy losses.

Try to find stocks with low correlations to each other.

In the example above, I ignored the impact of dealing costs (and these can be material in CFDs), the bid-offer spread and the interest debits on the CFDs. However, I have also ignored the interest that can be earned on the cash extracted.

Now let's have a look at a classic trade you can do using CFDs – buying an undervalued share and shorting a similar overvalued one.

4. Pairs Trading

Hedge funds have exuded glamour for many years, although this has perhaps become a bit tarnished of late as some of their techniques have been exposed as flawed. This example is, however, one classic way that the original hedge funds used to trade – still valid today. The strategy is sometimes known as *long/short equity* or *pairs trading*.

The idea is to profit from the narrowing of a disparity in the stock market rating of two similar companies. As an investor, you might, for example, believe that BT is cheap relative to Vodafone. BT sells on a dividend yield of 12% while Vodafone sells on a yield of 6%. You believe that this disparity should even itself out over a period of time.

A relatively low risk way of profiting from this would be to do a matched pairs trade using CFDs – shorting Vodafone and going long of BT in equal money amounts.

The argument against this type of trading is that your *dealing costs will be higher*, with two lots of commission and two bid-offer spreads to surmount before you reach profit. In the case of a CFD, the position is mitigated slightly because the financing credit on the short position will partly offset the financing cost of the long position.

The big plus point, however, is that this strategy ought (in theory at least) to mean that you are insulated from the ups and downs in the market. In the case of the Vodafone/BT example, if the market as a whole rises, or falls, the effect on your exposure will be neutral. In that event, both stocks should rise or fall more or less in tandem.

What you are interested in here is a change in the relative valuations of the stocks, not their absolute levels. That is how you make money from pairs trading. We'll see *exactly* how in a minute, but first, let's look at the requirements for doing a trade like this.

Chart 5.1: Vodafone's share price vs BT's (Vodafone is thicker line)

© ShareScope

The chart shows that BT and Vodafone's share prices have historically converged and diverged, providing opportunities for pairs trading between, for example, December 2002 and November 2005 and from the end of 2007 onwards. Note that very recently the gap opened up in 2008 has now closed with BT currently standing at around 100p and Vodafone at 132p.

Pairs trading requirements

We need to have a few conditions in place.

1. You need to check with your CFD broker that appropriate pairs of stocks are actually available.

2. It's important to remember that the trades must be matched at the outset in terms of their money value.

Control of costs is very important

What is important in pairs trading, though, is to make sure your dealing costs are at a minimum. It's unfortunate that individual stock futures are no longer available, because pairs-trading using CFDs is a more expensive exercise. However, you do get an interest credit on your short side trade, and even though this will not completely offset the debit on your long side trade, because the interest rate used will be higher in the case of the latter, it does mitigate the costs somewhat.

Dealing spreads are relatively narrow. But commission on CFDs can be an important consideration. Nonetheless serious private investors now have no option but to use CFDs for this type of trade.

Risk

Pairs trading isn't without risk. The stock you have bought might issue a profit warning, or it could bid for the stock you have shorted (about the worst possible combination of events since the ratings will diverge rather than converge if this happens!), but generally risk is minimised.

Let's have a look at a concrete example.

Example 5.5: Pairs trading (Vodafone v BT)

Here's the theory.

Say we take our original idea that Vodafone is dear (on a yield basis) at 130p and BT is cheap (on a yield basis) with its price also at 130p. I am using these somewhat historical prices because they illustrate the point. You think that the market will eventually come round to your way of thinking that their valuations will converge.

Because the prices are currently almost identical, selling the amount of Vodafone shares as a CFD for each amount of BT shares you buy as a CFD, you should be able to profit from the expected adjustment in the market ratings as expressed by the yield basis on the shares. If the market goes down as a whole, this needn't affect your profit from the trade, because the overvalued stock should drop more, leaving you in pocket.

Let's say, for instance, you buy 1000 BT shares as a CFD and sell 1000 Vodafone as a CFD at around 130p in each case. Assume now that the market drops 5%. BT drops from 130p to 128p but Vodafone falls proportionately further from 130p to 110p.

On the basis of the requirement to stump up 20% margin you have to pledge roughly £260 for each side of the trade.

The 20p fall in the price of Vodafone translates into a gain on the short side of the trade of £200.

The 2p drop in BT means that your long position in Vodafone has lost £20.

Because of the change in the relative price of the two stocks, you have a net gain of *£180* even though both stocks have gone down. Return on capital would be around 34.6% (£180 versus margin committed of £520).

However, these theoretical calculations exclude the impact of the bid-offer spread in both cases and the effect of dealing costs. As we can see from the more detailed accounting below, which uses the actual current market prices rather than our theoretical ones, the numbers in reality are a little different.

Pairs trade summary

Objective: profit from an adjustment in relative prices of Vodafone and BT.

Initial prices

Company	Cash	CFD
Vodafone	128-30	128-130
BT	130-31	130-131

Action: using CFDs, go short of Vodafone and long of BT.

Opening position

Position	Amount	Type	Stock	Price	Amount	Margin(£)
Sell	1000	CFD	Vodafone	128	1280	256
Buy	1000	CFD	BT	131	1310	262

Market: Vodafone stock falls to 110; BT stock falls to 128

Action: Vodafone CFD bought back at 111; BT CFD sold at 127

Profit/loss

	P/L(£)	Calculation
Gain on short Vodafone	170	1 x 17p x 1000
Loss on long BT	-40	1 x 4p x 1000
Commission (approx)	-13	2 x 0.25% x £2590
Net profit	117	170 – 40 – 13
Return on investment	22.6%	117/518 (518 was the total margin)

The margin element inherent here allows you to profit from quite small changes in the relative value of the two stocks. But you need to keep an eagle eye on dealing costs to make sure you can profit from the trade. In the example above, the impact of the spread and commission reduced the theoretical return from the trade.

I have also assumed that interest costs on the long trade are cancelled out by interest credits on the short trade, whereas this would not be precisely the case in practice. Nonetheless the example shows in principle how a trade like this can work.

5. Relative Value Trades

Another lower risk way of trading using CFDs is betting on the relative performance of a stock against the market. Let's say you believe that the market as a whole is overvalued but that defensive stocks, like food companies, are going to do much better than the index over the coming months. We'll use the example of Unilever.

Example 5.6: Relative value trade (Unilever v FTSE 100)

The way to play this view is to buy a defensive stock, Unilever, as a CFD and short the index. This means that you should benefit from the stock's relative strength against the market, irrespective of the size of the fall in the market. You may believe the market is going to crash, but even if it only drops a small amount, this strategy should work, as this example shows.

The conventional index futures contract is £10 per index point, meaning that the FTSE 100 future has a current underlying value (at the time of writing) of around £40,000 (index currently – in October 2008 – around 4000. Assuming the FTSE 100 is at 4000 this means the underlying value is £40,000. Assuming margin is 10%, we can buy or sell one contract for £4000 down.

Chart 5.2: Unilever share price vs FTSE 100 (FTSE 100 is thicker line)

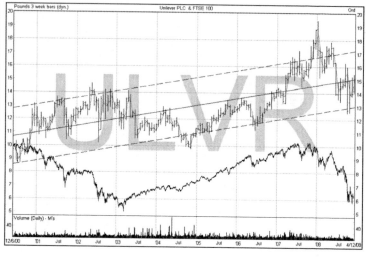

© ShareScope

The chart illustrates the defensive nature of Unilever, with the shares holding up very well during the 2000 to 2003 bear phase in the market and also proving relatively resilient during the period of market weakness in 2008. This makes Unilever ideal for this type of trading strategy.

Rather neatly, because it makes the example easy to understand, when the manuscript of this book was compiled Unilever was (in October 2008) priced around 1336p per share, so that a CFD in 3000 shares was worth £40,080. This more or less matched the value of a FTSE 100 futures contract at the time. The point to bear in mind is that, as with a pairs trade, you need to have parity in terms of underlying total contract value for each side of the trade.

In this example we're going to look at what happens if Unilever remains unchanged, but the index falls 250 points – in other words, if Unilever outperforms the index the way we expect it to.

Relative value trade summary

Objective: low-risk profit from appreciation of a defensive stock versus the market

Initial prices

	Cash	CFD or Future
Unilever	1335-37	1335-38
FTSE 100	4000	4000-4005

Action: go long of Unilever and short of FTSE 100

Opening position

Position	Amount	Inst/Expiry	Contract	Price	Amount	Margin(£)
Buy	3000	CFD	Unilever	1338	40,140	4014
Sell	1	Dec Future	FTSE 100	4000	40,000	4000

Market: FTSE 100 falls 250 points; Unilever no change

Action: Unilever CFD sold at 1335; FTSE 100 future bought back at 3750

Profit/loss

	P/L (£)	Calculation
Loss on Unilever CFD	-90	3 x 1000 x 3p (spread)
Profit on FTSE future	2500	250 x £10
Dealing costs on FTSE futures	-20	2 x £10 per contract
Dealing costs of CFD	-400	2 x 0.25% of consideration
Net profit	1990	(-90-400) + (2500-20)
Return on investment	24.8%	1990/8014 (i.e. combined margin)

CFD or futures?

Trades like this can in principle also be done using either CFDs or spread bets, both of which give more flexibility than futures. This is because of the ability to have more precise tailoring of the quantities used in each case. They may, however, attract higher dealing costs, and/or bigger percentage margin requirements. Once again, all of these costs should be carefully checked out ahead of time. They can be a significant drain on the potential profit you can make.

6. Hedging

Another way of using CFDs is to employ them, quite literally, to hedge your bets.

Hedging is really like insurance. You use a short CFD or a down spread bet to protect an existing holding in the event of a price fall. This allows you to leave the original holding undisturbed (avoiding a possible capital gains tax bill if you had sold), but make an offsetting profit on the hedge if the underlying price falls.

Here's an example.

Example 5.7: Hedging using CFDs, Vodafone

Background

It's 2006. Let's say that you bought your current holding of 10,000 Vodafone shares when the company first spun out of the old Racal Electronics business in the late 1980s. It's a long-term holding and you have a big capital gain. Imagine the shares are 200p, and your cost price is 50p. You think the market is overvalued and that if it falls sharply in price, then Vodafone will do too. You don't want to sell and suffer capital gains tax on your holding, but you want to avoid being caught in a market slump.

Initial parameters

Simply sell 10,000 Vodafone as a CFD at 200p. (This matches your exposure to the underlying shares exactly and let's assume, because Vodafone is not very volatile, margin is 10% and that the position therefore ties up only £2000 of capital).

For the sake of argument let's say that Vodafone falls from 200p to 150p.

Result

1. If you had sold your share holding at 200p, you would have had a capital gain of 150p a share, and ended up paying 18% (27p) of that amount in capital gains tax.

2. After deducting the tax you would have been, in effect, getting only 173p for your sale at 200p. (That's more than half the decline in the price gone in tax!)

As it is, because you are using a CFD trade you recoup your loss without disturbing the underlying holding.

Let's look in detail at precisely how this hedging strategy works using a CFD, assuming, say, the drop in price is expected to occur over a period of about three months.

Example: Hedging using CFDs

To recap:

1. You hold 10,000 Vodafone shares bought at 50p a share.

2. The shares are currently priced at 200p.

3. You expect the price to fall to 150p over the next three months.

You want to use a CFD to hedge this position. Here's how it would work if the price fall happens as you expect.

Table 5.4: Hedging using a CFD

Item	Hold Shares	Short CFD
Holding	10,000	10,000
Underlying value @ 200p	£20,000	£20,000
Capital employed	£20,000	£2000 (margin)
Commission (0.25% each way)	n/a	-£100
Interest @ 4% (90 days)	n/a	£200
Value @150p	£15,000	£15,000
P&L	-£5000	+£5100
Net result	+100 (excluding impact of spreads)	

In other words, the loss in the shares has more than been made up for by the gain on the CFD, which also includes interest on the short position. Bear in mind though, that there may be capital gains tax to pay (£920 in the worst case scenario) on the gain in the CFD. However, had the whole holding been sold, the CGT bill would have been £2700 (18% of your profit of 150p a share) on the original holding.

The influence of tax

Tax considerations can be an important factor. Although in this example the CGT payable on the CFD would be a lot less than it would be if you had sold the shareholding outright (18% of £5112 rather than 18% of £15,000), it still lessens the impact of your insurance.

Though a spread bet might mean the hedge cost a few pennies more, it could therefore, depending on your capital gains tax position, make more sense to put on the hedge using a down spread bet.

That way, you wouldn't earn interest on your short, but equally you wouldn't pay commission or CGT either.

What happens if you turn out to be wrong, and Vodafone's shares in this example don't fall but continue to rise?

Unless you remove the hedge, it works in reverse and deprives you of the benefit of the rise. You don't lose money on a net basis, but you forgo a gain.

7. Using CFDs for Adjusting Asset Allocation

Asset allocation is a much neglected discipline. Many private investors tend to focus on stock picking. Most individuals overestimate their ability to beat the market by picking stocks. Having a few winners in a rising market tends to produce the illusion that the game of investing is easier than it is in reality. Many investors found this out the hard way in October 2008, when the market crashed spectacularly.

Asset allocation, by contrast, focuses less on individual stocks and more on the overall amounts invested in categories such as equities, bonds, cash, property and alternative investments. It has been estimated that simply getting these proportions correct at the right time can represent as much as 90% of overall performance, with decisions on individual investments playing a relatively minor role.

ETFs

The advent of exchange traded funds (in effect index funds that trade like shares) allows investors to tailor their exposure precisely. Exchange traded funds exist for a plethora of equity indices at home and abroad, but also for sectors, for bullion, and for government bonds in different currencies and for corporate bonds. These produce income and have low management charges.

You can use exchange traded funds to tweak asset allocation decisions on the basis of short-term considerations. For those with long-term share portfolios that need not be disturbed, however, CFDs in bonds and gold can be used to take advantage of short-term opportunities in the market. You can use them to dilute exposure to equities at times of market crisis. This is a variant of the hedging tactics described earlier in this chapter.

Equally, those with a conservative outlook and a heavy position in bonds, cash and alternative investments might at times feel strongly that they could profit by either being long or short of the equity market for a brief period. CFDs are an ideal way of giving effect to this view, particularly given that any surplus cash can be pledged as collateral for a margin account, as the following brief illustration shows.

Example 5.8: Using CFDs to adjust asset allocation

The starting point is that you have the following:

1. £100,000 portfolio, invested 50% in gilts; 25% in cash; 25% in a FTSE 100 index fund.

2. You believe the index, currently 4000, is set for a sharp rise.

3. You wish to increase your equity exposure on a temporary basis.

Action: Assuming 10% margin, for collateral of £5000 (easily pledged from your cash), you can triple your equity market exposure by buying a CFD with an underlying consideration of £50,000.

Scenario: Market rises by 25% over three months from 4000 to 5000. Gilts remain unchanged. You close the CFD trade after the market's strong rise.

Result: The difference in performance of your portfolio (ignoring costs for the moment) would have been as follows:

Portfolio Item	Original Value (£)	After mkt rise	After mkt rise
		No CFD	With CFD
Gilts	50,000	50,000	50,000
Cash	25,000	25,000	25,000
Index Fund	25,000	31,250	31,250
Index CFD profit			12,500
Total	100,000	106,250	118,750

The result of this simple exercise is that the underlying performance of a conservative portfolio has been tripled (or slightly less than tripled after costs are taken into account) as a result of temporarily increasing equity exposure via a CFD.

Commission on the purchase and sale of the CFD would (at 0.25% of consideration) be £250, and there is interest to pay, which might be a further £500 (assuming interest is debited at 4%). This would still leave the overall performance well into double figures in percentage terms versus the 6% or so gain if no action had been taken.

It perhaps goes without saying that such a view only works this way if the market rises strongly and you anticipated the gain correctly. More modest market gains, or worse, no gains at all, risk any outperformance being eaten up by commission and interest costs.

It also follows that, by going short, you could use an index CFD to mitigate your portfolio's equity exposure to an overvalued stock market, if you believed that a major setback was imminent.

8. Other Strategies – Exploiting Ex-dividend Anomalies

The fact that net dividends are credited to a CFD account on the ex-dividend day (rather than payment day) creates opportunities for nimble traders to exploit 'stickiness' in the market when it comes to adjusting ex-dividend prices. It doesn't happen on every occasion, but it is possible for traders to exploit those occasions where it does.

A list of stocks going ex-dividend in the following week can usually be found in the 'week ahead' sections of the press or financial websites, from the London Stock Exchange dividend calendar, or from company results announcements. The norm is for the ex-dividend date to be the Wednesday immediately preceding the record date for a pending dividend payment.

While market makers normally adjust for ex-dividend amounts, it's often the case that, in a neutral market, the shares will open ex-dividend without having fully adjusted for the impact of the dividend, partly perhaps because technical support levels may have propped up the price, or because some ill informed investors buy because they think they are getting a bargain.

The way to take advantage of this using a CFD is to buy the stock near the close on the day prior to the ex-dividend day and to sell at or very close to the open the following morning. Your account will be credited with the net dividend and you may be able to deal at a price that does not reflect the full amount of the dividend credit. If so, returns on trades like this are improved because of the geared up nature of CFD trading. Costs need to be taken into account, of course.

The following example shows how it works.

Example 5.9: Dividend trading opportunity – Cable & Wireless

Initial parameters

- Cable & Wireless goes ex a 5p net dividend on 6th June 2008.
- The CFD price is 167-167.5.
- You buy 5000 shares at 167.5 as a CFD.
- On the next trading day the shares open at 166-166.5
- You bank the net dividend and sell at 166.

Implications

The cash flows for this trade are as follows:

Loss on CFD position due to price change	-£75
Commission on purchase and sale	-£16.75 and -£16.60 = -£33.75
Dividend on 5000 shares (at 5p)	+£250

Result

Ignoring the small amount of a daily interest on a position that is only open overnight this gives a profit after costs of £141.25. Assuming 20% margin, capital employed is £1675 and the return on the trade is 8.4%. Commission and the bid-offer spread combined amount to 1.175p per share, hence any ex-dividend price adjustment less than 3.825p means that the trade will yield a positive return.

It takes experience to know how and when to make these trades work, but the fact is that anomalies like this do crop up from time to time. It's unwise to attempt trades like this in anything other than trendless markets. They are a risky business in markets that are falling.

The advantage of trading around an ex-dividend date is, however, that it is by definition in the immediate *aftermath* of a results announcement. In the normal course of events this means the chances of a bearish announcement from the company are relatively low, and recent trading results are already fully reflected in the price.

Afterword

Let's have a look at the key points we've learnt in this chapter.

There are several different types of trade you can place: straight long or short; stop-loss; cash extraction; pairs trading; relative value trading; and hedging, as well as other variants such as using CFDs to change asset allocation and to take advantage of anomalies in 'ex-dividend' adjustments.

CFDs work well for relative value trades and pairs trading because of the interest earned element on the short side of the trade. Against that, commission may be higher than for futures, although margin might be a little less. Margin percentages are likely to be highest on spread bets and least on futures or possibly CFDs, depending on the firm you use and the stock or stocks involved.

In reality, however, in the case of trades in individual stocks, private investors have little option but to use CFDs (or spread bets) to effect futures-type trades like this.

Either way, you do need to spend time before you commit to a trade working out the exact costs and where they will arise. You also need to know what the break-even points of the trade will be. Part of this process is also to analyse price charts to work out the size of the move you can realistically expect in each component of a trade. Then work out what a move like this means for profits and your return on capital after dealing costs and spreads have been taken into account. This is the subject of a later chapter.

In the first instance, however, we need to spell out in rather greater detail some of the necessary skills, disciplines and techniques you need to adopt when managing your trading account.

6
Trading Disciplines

W e've spent quite a bit of time so far looking at the different strategies you can employ when using CFDs for purposes other than simple geared-up speculation. But discipline and planning are equally important.

CFDs trades are inherently volatile. If the trade goes the wrong way you will get margin calls and may have to sell other assets to meet it. So buying and holding is not a choice you can make here. You need to have a plan of action for your trading, have a method for monitoring it, and a trigger to make you act decisively if it looks as though things are going wrong.

You need to be able to use various investment tools, including technical analysis software. These can help you define the likely risks and rewards of the trades before you initiate them. Market timing software can also help.

We'll cover all of these aspects in turn later in this chapter. But first, here are some basic guidelines for your trading.

Trading Rules

The problem of emotion

One of the problems with trading is that emotion gets in the way. If you let it take hold, it will wreck your chances of making and keeping a decent return.

One way of avoiding being gripped by emotion is a simple one. It is to write down in a notebook, when you make the trade, what your thoughts are and what the specific reasons for doing the trade were at the time, and what the financial objectives of the trade are.

Then as events unfold you can return to your notes and act accordingly. Either you cut your losses if things go wrong or circumstances change, or you take your profits if the trade works out as you intended. The last point may seem obvious, but it is not unknown for traders to be overcome by the greed for greater profits and, by holding on, miss the chance to get out. This is particularly important with some of the strategies we've looked at because of the limited time at your disposal to extract a profit.

This method is a simple way of eliminating the emotion that can disrupt your thought processes and lead to losses or missed opportunities. In reality it is just another way of saying that any deal you do should be monitored throughout its life. It's particularly important with investments that can be volatile or which have a time limit. You need to keep your wits about you. Take the events of October 2008, when the market dropped very sharply as a result of the crisis of confidence in the banking sector.

These events suggest that you also need to be extremely well attuned to the current state of the market and in particular to the risks that it can pose. These risks may override all other logical valuation considerations on individual shares. Firm and rapid action is needed in a CFD portfolio if the market background deteriorates sharply.

Derivatives are not for 'buy and hold'

One of the great trading rules of the markets is that if anything causes you to doubt the wisdom of holding a particular position, the trade should be closed without delay. This has been expressed in other words in that famous stock market aphorism:

if in doubt, get out

In a derivative like a CFD that you've bought for a speculation, this rule is a particularly important one to follow. There is no point, as you might do with a stock, holding on in the hope that better times will eventually come. Even in conventional stock market trading, this is usually a bad idea anyway.

Flexibility

The next cardinal rule is not to stick too dogmatically to a particular stance on the market. I've already said you should try and establish buying and selling points in advance, but don't adhere to them rigidly if circumstances look to have changed permanently.

If the outlook for a particular stock appears to have improved (results are better than expected; there are rumours of takeover in the offing; or a bid is announced) it may be wise to abandon a previous profit lock-in point and institute a higher one. This can be done in the CFD market (as we found in the previous chapter) by using a trailing stop-loss rather than a conventional one. The same thing works in reverse if the fundamentals for the company worsen. It pays to be flexible.

Cut losses

For the few trades that go spectacularly right, there will be many that are unexciting or just bad. The aim of all trading is to minimise the losses that occur when things go wrong and to maximise the profits of the ones that succeed. Cutting losses relatively quickly is a vital element in this. Equally, don't get too greedy. The legendary financier Bernard Baruch was once asked how he came to be so rich. His answer was:

by always selling too early

You can learn a lot from studying past losses in detail to work out why they occurred. All investors, even experienced ones, make mistakes. The important point is that, if you study your past mistakes, you can discipline yourself not to repeat them.

Keep it simple

Finally, keep it simple. You might want to have a few different trades open at the same time, but you must remain focused. In order to keep your risk to acceptable levels you might want to make sure that there isn't an obvious correlation between your trades.

There's not much point, for example, in having two open CFD trades on stocks or indices that might move in the same direction at the same time. If you want to speculate on the movement in the NASDAQ market through a CFD, it makes sense not to have another trade open in a similar technology-heavy index. In other words, make sure your risks are diversified. Even this may not be infallible protection. In times of stock market crisis all markets tend to move together in one direction, whatever their relative merits on logical grounds.

Golden Rules of Trading

1. Keep a note of your reasons for a trade, and its exit price.

2. If in doubt get out, but run your profits.

3. Don't let hope get in the way of realism.

4. Don't be greedy.

5. Be flexible if circumstances change.

6. Cut your losses quickly, preferably by using stop-losses.

7. Learn from your mistakes. Measure your performance honestly.

8. Diversify, but recognise that in extreme circumstances, it may not be enough.

9. Don't trade too often. Only trade when you are convinced conditions are right.

Money management

There are also some basic rules that fall under the heading of what American investors call *money management*. Let's have a look at them and the impact they should have on your trading plan.

Keep losses small

This sounds obvious. But there is a simple mathematical reason why you should do this. Cutting a loss on an investment that has dropped 10% means you only have to have a gain of 11% on a subsequent investment to recoup the loss. If you don't cut your loss until the share has dropped 30%, you need a 43% rise in the next investment to recoup your loss. If the investment halves, your next investment must double to get back the loss. And so on. So have your pain barrier, either in percentage terms or a money amount, and stick to it.

Where you can, use stop-losses

Stop-losses are automatically triggered orders that close out a trade when a certain price is hit. When you speculate using volatile, highly-geared investments like CFDs, you should always trade with stop-loss orders in place. CFD brokers will guarantee to execute stop-loss orders. It's hard to do this in normal shares.

Don't risk too much

Accidents happen. Many trades make losses. It's often the case that only two trades out of ten will make a really solid return. The way to make money is to avoid the big losing trades. So don't bet your shirt on a single throw of the dice. Some traders say you should never risk more than 2% of your capital on a single trade. That seems to me to be too restrictive. But certainly the amount in question should be well under 10% of your capital. Divide your total capital by, say, 15 and don't bet more than this on a single deal – even with a stop-loss in place.

Make sure your capital is adequate

CFDs entail having a minimum amount of capital invested or collateral available to meet margin calls. Make sure that you have adequate resources to fund the account and that you have plenty left over for margin calls. You don't want to be forced into selling assets you may not want to part with.

Never average down

Averaging down is committing more capital to a losing position to get the average book cost down. It is throwing good money after bad. You are increasing your exposure to a trade that has gone bad. On the other hand, adding to a winning trade can be a good idea.

Know when to sell

This is a hard one. Many investors have great difficulty deciding when to get out. Losses are easy. Cut a loss quickly, when it hits your pain barrier. With trades that are making money, most advocate selling if one of the following happens:

1. If circumstances generally change

2. After a profit warning (if long)

3. After an unexpected management change (if long)

4. If a share falls more than 15% from an all time high (if long)

5. If the market moves against you on very high volume

These rules apply to CFD trades in individual stocks and markets. Focus on stop-losses.

Measure your gains and losses

It's worth looking at your performance in a couple of ways. The first is to look at the ratio of profits to losses on your trades. Take all your winning trades and average them. Take all your losing trades and average them. Divide the average profit into the average loss. Then look at how many trades by number are profitable and how many are losers. Divide one number into the other. This is called the accuracy ratio.

These ratios have a simple message. If your accuracy rate is low, you need to improve your trade selection. If your profit-loss ratio is too low, you need to examine whether you are hanging on to losing trades too long, or taking profits too early.

Trading Tips for CFDs

You need to be aware that there are not only general trading and money management rules, but also ones for specific instruments like CFDs.

So here are a few pointers on trading, specific to CFDs.

Avoid opening and closing sessons

Avoid trading at the beginning and end of the trading day.

Why is this so?

It's simple. End of day book-squaring exercises by professional traders distort share prices and the index value at the close. For the same reason prices set during the first hour of trading may be unrepresentative of the true level that will be established later. If you are trading CFDs (or for that matter futures or spread bets) in shares or indices, avoid trading at these times.

An exception is in the case of the illustration in the previous chapter relating to trading around ex-dividend dates, when opening a trade at the very end of the day and closing just after the open on the following (ex-dividend) day is the essence of the trade and in this instance minimises the risk that the trade will be disrupted by extraneous market events.

Understand the influence of the US

Foreign indices, particularly the Dow Jones in the US, affect the way the FTSE 100 index moves in the afternoon UK time. The FTSE 100 index is therefore really only 'its own person' between about 9am and 1.30pm, before US index futures markets begin trading actively.

Understand your broker's order system

A stop-loss order is often not automatically cancelled if you close the trade yourself. It's important, when doing a closing trade, to also cancel the stop-loss order at the same time. You need to check the firm's policy on this before you place the trade. This applies to any CFD provider that offers guaranteed stop-losses, although some do offer the facility whereby stop-losses can be cancelled automatically in this eventuality.

Summary of trading tips for CFDs

1. Avoid trading at the beginning and end of the day (ex-dividend trades excepted).

2. Trade the UK index in the morning.

3. If you close a trade early, cancel the stop-loss order too.

Developing Your Plan by Looking at Your Assets

How you use CFDs depends on your starting point.

In short, the action you take and the instrument you use will depend on the size of your investment portfolio, your requirements for income from those investments, your appetite for risk, the extent to which your assets are already diversified and a number of other factors.

Know where the volatility really is

We saw in the last chapter how judicious use of CFDs at key points in the market can help adjust your exposure. But there is another aspect to this. It is that some investors might fight shy of using CFDs in ways that could potentially be beneficial, because they become too focused on the inherent volatility of CFDs in a long-only or short-only context and fail to see this volatility in the context of their broader assets and the volatility of their other investments.

There are countless examples where investors ignore the gearing and risk that might be present elsewhere in their portfolio and focus too tightly on the volatility and risk in a small part of their overall investment exposure.

For instance, buying a £250,000 property on a 90% mortgage is essentially the same decision as buying a CFD on the index, or let's say, a CFD on a major property investment company or real estate investment trust with a consideration of £250,000 and margin of 10%. The only difference is that the mortgaged property is a physical asset that you can live in or rent to someone else.

The gearing in property investments

While a property can be rented, an index or share CFD will also pay a dividend, so the effective differences are few. Property investors who rent out their properties often underestimate the additional costs that deplete the return (void periods when there are no tenants, maintenance costs, regular charges that tenants don't pay, bad debts and so on).

People are usually comfortable buying property on this basis (some might say we are too comfortable doing it). But – capital gains tax considerations aside – many would instinctively shy away from doing a trade with broadly equivalent risk using a CFD. The feeling that we all know something about property by virtue of living in our own homes is sometimes a dangerous illusion.

Risk is to be managed, not avoided completely

By the same token, cash-rich, pending retirees may tend to be cautious about their money, when small calculated risks might be worthwhile.

Take a 60-year old investor whose pension fund of £800,000 has just matured and, pending benefits being taken, will simply earn interest at the market rate (say around 4%). Assume that he also owns an unmortgaged investment property worth a further £800,000 and has an investment portfolio of £400,000 split 50/50 between gilts and equities.

This investor has extremely limited exposure to the ups and down of the equity market, approximately 10% of the total portfolio of pension, property and other investments. The stance being taken here is extremely low risk and low return. It may, in fact, not give an appropriate level of exposure to equities that would mitigate the corrosive effect of inflation on the portfolio's cash and fixed income investments.

We need not advocate (and I am not) that this investor starts playing around with CFDs using his pension fund cash, although CFDs can be in fact be included as part of a SIPP. But simply that the risks being run with modest CFD exposure need to be placed in the context of an individual's total investable assets. It's normal to exclude a person's main residence from this calculation and arguably one should also perhaps exclude that portion of the pension fund that cannot be taken as a tax free lump sum. But the important point is to look at one's assets in total and not simply at those assets directly exposed to the stock market. The overriding need is to be aware that market disasters can occur, but so can opportunities, and to take risks that one feels comfortable with and commensurate to one's overall investable assets.

Each investor is different. So before deciding whether or not to use CFDs as part of your trading, you need to make a clear and objective assessment of your current portfolio in the broadest sense and your aims and objectives in terms of capital growth, income, and risk.

There are further points. One relates to CGT. Capital gains on major holdings need to be assessed to see whether a hedging strategy should be employed. Once you have done this, the appropriate strategy and the tools to use to achieve it should become obvious. Even though gains on them are themselves subject to CFDs, they can be used legitimately as part of hedging strategy, as explained in an earlier chapter.

7

Timing Your Trades

W hen you are trading in CFDs, you will need to make a judgement about the likely price movement of the underlying share or index on which they are based. Though CFDs, unlike futures and spread bets, have no time limit involved, the interest element on a long CFD means that you can't really think of it as an investment you make indefinitely, if the expected move that gave rise to the trade doesn't materialise.

I'm labouring this point because it does mean that you need to have a reasonably precise idea about the potential magnitude of future rises and falls in the price of the shares or other security underlying the CFD, and the speed with which these changes might happen. The only way to determine this with any degree of accuracy (and even here the element of accuracy isn't perfect) is by studying price charts.

This is true of anything you trade. The long-term value of anything you trade will ultimately be governed by fundamentals. With shares it might be their profits, balance sheet and growth outlook. For interest rates it might be money supply and GDP growth. And so on. But it can take a very long time for these fundamentals to assert themselves and, as has frequently been observed, the market can stay irrational longer than a trader can remain solvent. Judgements about timing and short-term price movements – whether trading shares, bonds, foreign exchange, commodities and stock market indices – need to be made taking into account the indicators contained in the price charts.

The study of price charts and the attempt to use them to predict or explain price movements is known as *technical analysis*.

Basic technical analysis

Price charts and some of the signals they produce work partly because traders expect them to work and act accordingly. But they also work because they reflect a part of human nature.

Support and resistance levels

One aspect of this, for example, is that investors and traders find comfort in familiar patterns. Another is the reluctance of many investors to take a loss, or the reluctance to sell for less than a high water mark established in the recent past. Arguably, these tendencies are meaningless distortions that should not necessarily mean much in an ideal world of rational behaviour. But the fact is that they do exist, and produce distinctive patterns on charts.

Let's look at a specific example to explain what we mean. If a share price has traded for a long time between 250p and 350p, and it's currently fallen to close to 250p, it's reasonable to suppose that many traders will be looking to buy at that point, and that buying pressure will lift the price. If it then moves up towards 350p, traders will look to sell, depressing the price. The second order effect is that a trader who missed out buying at 250p or selling at 350p will be doubly determined not to miss the boat when the same pattern is repeated in the future.

This is why many charts move in regular patterns and produce behaviour that is self-reinforcing. It is also why technical analysts set so much store by these so-called **support and resistance levels**. A *support level* in the example above would be at 250p, where a fall in price to this level would produce an influx of buyers to support the price. The *resistance level* would be at 350p, where any attempted rise in price beyond this point would be resisted by an influx of sellers, many perhaps who missed outselling at this point previously.

Trends

The same factors govern the way some share prices move up or down in a defined trend. In a classic uptrend each successive short-term high and low in the share price will be higher than the previous one. Joining the successive highs and lows will produce *trendlines* that are virtually parallel. The share price will meander ever higher within these limits. A downtrend is the same situation in reverse, where successive highs and lows are below the previous ones.

Many traders simply act as trend-followers, opening a trade and riding the trend until it peters out or reverses decisively. But it takes experience to know which are the best and most reliable trends to follow.

Moving averages

One problem many traders have is to distinguish between random minute by minute or day by day fluctuations in price that are of little significance and those that represent the real underlying movement in the price. One way of eliminating this random chatter is to using **moving averages**. A ten-day moving average, for example, will take will take the average closing price for ten successive trading days and work out the simple arithmetic mean price. The following trading day the new closing price will be added, the oldest of the ten dropped off, and the average recalculated. When this series of averages is plotted on a graph, the effect is to iron out the very short-term fluctuations and produce a smoother curve that better represents the underlying trend.

Technical analysts use moving averages in a variety of ways, but there are several recognised combinations. One, for example, is to plot the normal price chart in conjunction with the 20-day or 50-day moving average, with trigger points being where the shorter term indicator changes direction and moves up or down through the longer term average. Another is to plot two moving averages of different length on the same chart (say a 30-day and a 90-day moving average). Here the same rule applies, with traders looking for points at which the shorter term average crosses the longer term one when both are moving in the same direction.

The problem that traders have with devices like this is that the signals they produce are often only produced after a significant movement in the price has taken place and the best opportunity to trade has been missed.

Support and resistance, trendlines, and breaks through moving averages

As is probably clear already, technical analysis is a huge subject. There are many books you can read about it, some of which are listed in the next chapter. There are books to cover all of the main concepts and indicators in some detail.

But it is worth keeping in mind that support and resistance, trendlines, and breaks through moving averages are arguably the most widely used indicators and remain important for shorter term traders because they can provide predictions of the speed and extent of particular movements. Support and resistance levels in particular are of especial importance when it comes to placing stop-losses.

This is because the concepts of support and resistance are not infallible indicators. These arbitrary price levels can be broken through on occasions. A break-up through a resistance level to a new high, for example, might possibly be followed by a substantial further movement in the same direction. In this instance, it would be a trading disaster to be short of a CFD. Traders therefore position stop-losses just above significant resistance levels (if short) or just below significant support levels (if long), so that the position is closed quickly if the support or resistance level is unexpectedly breached.

Patterns

Price charts produce many different patterns and over the years technical analysts have attempted a sort of taxonomy of the patterns and what they presage in subsequent price action. Many have evocative names: flags; pennants; double bottoms; double tops; triple bottoms; triple tops; head and shoulders; reverse head and shoulders; saucer bottoms; accumulation; distribution and so on.

Technical analysis literature can explain more of the detail about these particular patterns. From the point of the CFD trader, however, the point to remember is that some of these patterns take a long time to form and may not be especially helpful when it comes to assessing the potential for a trade that may only be intended to last a matter of days or a few weeks.

A further point to make here is that in the case of major changes of direction, such as occur in the case of double tops, double bottoms, head and shoulders patterns and other similar indicators, the signal is reinforced if the changes take place on heavy volume. Trading volume at a time of major changes of market direction is an important indicator.

Combining technical analysis and knowledge of fundamentals

It is also important that CFD traders bear in mind that indicators that relate to fundamentals can and should be used in conjunction with conventional technical analysis to identify opportunities for profitable trading. We have already identified in the previous chapter, for instance, the opportunities that can be presented as a result of ex-dividend announcements. It is worthwhile looking at technical patterns in a particular share, for example, in conjunction with known key dates in the company calendar: AGM dates, dates of results announcements, date the company enters a close period and might therefore issue a trading statement.

For interest rate related CFDs, key dates might be those related to known dates of central bank announcements related to interest rates, release dates of key economic numbers covering inflation, economic growth, unemployment and the like. For each CFD trade you make, you need to know what the key announcements are likely to be and when precisely they are expected to occur.

Before going on to look at some more advanced technical indicators, the following table is a summary of some of the indicators discussed already, and the price potential they suggest.

Table 7.1: Some basic technical indicators and what they mean

Indicator	What happens	Next move in price
Trend channel	Price bounces off bottom	To top of channel
Trend channel	Price bounces off top	To bottom of channel
Support level	Price bounces up	Up to next resistance
Resistance level	Price bounces down	Down to next support
Head & Shoulders	Price falls through 'neckline'	'Neck to head' move down
Reverse H&S	Price rises through 'neckline'	'Neck to head' move up
200D MA	Price breaks up through avg	Up to next resistance
200D MA	Price breaks down through avg	Down to next support
20D and 50D MA	20D crosses 50D, both rising	Bullish (Golden Cross)
20D and 50D MA	20D crosses 50D, both falling	Bearish (Dead Cross)

The first of the following screenshots shows a long-term chart of the S&P 500 with a logarithmic scale and with a head and shoulders pattern clearly visible between September 1998 and July 2002, with a neckline around the 1000 mark. In percentage terms a fall of around 33% might have been expected once the neckline was broken. The actual fall was just over 20%.

A subsequent, though weaker, pattern between mid 2006 and mid 2008 might have been expected to result in a fall to just under the 1000 level, whereas in this case the fall has been much more marked. Both examples show that rules like this are not precise.

Chart 7.1: A chart of the S&P 500 showing two head & shoulders formations

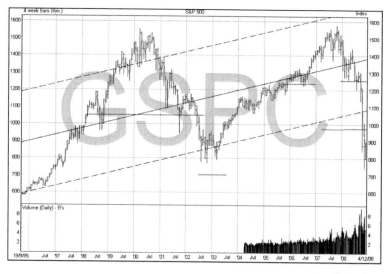

© ShareScope

The next chart shows regular trading patterns in AstraZeneca between £18 and £28 for several years both before and after recent market peaks. In the intervening period £28 became the bottom of a trading range that extended up to around £36. This shows how, once a pattern like this is observed and proves reliable, it might be possible to take a CFD position at the top or bottom of the trading range. AstraZeneca's current price of £25.61 is in the upper half of this trading range. Just under £20 has proved a consistent bottom for the AstraZeneca share price.

Chart 7.2: Cyclical trading pattern in AstraZeneca

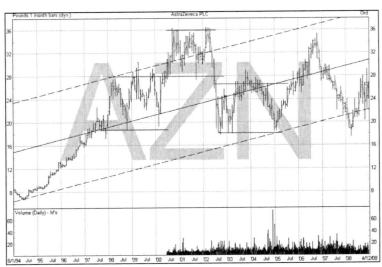

© ShareScope

More advanced technical indicators

Many investors in the past have been wont to dismiss technical analysis as an arcane discipline that does not really work when it comes to making valid investment decisions. While it is true that in the long term the fundamentals should guide all major investment decisions, CFD trading is essentially short term in nature. It should therefore make use of technical analysis as a vital aid, and in conjunction with other money management disciplines, to timing entry and exit points in trades.

To characterise technical analysis as unscientific is to misjudge the way it works. Many technical indicators are founded on valid statistical concepts and are calculated in a rigorous statistical fashion. Moving averages are a simple example of this idea at work. But there are more complex indicators too.

Confidence limits

Confidence limits (or confidence intervals) utilise the well-worn statistical concept of standard deviation and the degree to which this will predict, with measurable probability, that a price will remain within certain limits (specific multiples of standard deviation) on either side of a central long-term average.

The calculation process (least squares regression) produces a 'line of best fit' for a particular data series (let's say, a six month price history for a share). In theory, in this instance a share price should remain within plus or minus 1.96 standard deviations from the mean 95% of the time, or 2.58 standard deviations from the mean 99% of the time.

That doesn't mean to say of course that this is a complete certainty, but that – with appropriate safeguards such as stop-losses, and perhaps looked at in conjunction with other factors such as pre-existing support and resistance levels – it can be used to establish buying and selling points with a very great degree of accuracy.

Chart 7.3: Marks & Spencer

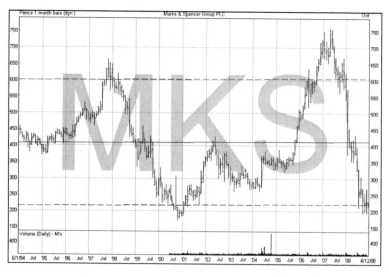

The chart shows that when M&S has risen above the 600p mark, the shares invariably retrace sharply. M&S has also tended to recover when the shares have fallen below the lower confidence limit of around 220p.

MACD

Devised in the 1960s, this is the Moving Average Convergence Divergence indicator – or MACD.

It combines two cycles, one with a relatively long amplitude combined with one of a shorter amplitude that acts as a trigger for buy and sell signals.

In the case of the MACD rather than use moving averages covering two different period lengths (14-day and 42-day averages for example, or 13-day and 26-day in some formulations – as in the chart) to perform this function, it does something rather more subtle. It calculates the moving averages for two time periods like this, but then computes a series of values for the difference between them, by subtracting one from the other. This is then plotted on a chart as the so-called 'main line'.

What is then done is to compute a moving average of main line over a relatively short period (perhaps seven days or nine days) to act as a trigger, with buying and selling signals being generated when the two lines cross under specific circumstances.

The MACD is plotted on a chart where zero is the equilibrium and buy signals are generated when the main line crosses up through the trigger line from below, with sell signals generated when the main line crosses down through the trigger line from above. Some schools of thought also read the crossing of the main line through the zero axis from below as a buy signal and the crossing through zero from above as a sell signal.

One problem with MACD is that when a particular market or share is directionless, the signals become confused. As an indicator it is best used to spot a change of direction after a sustained trend has been established for a significant length of time.

This can be seen in operation in the chart of United Utilities.

Chart 7.4: United Utilities MACD

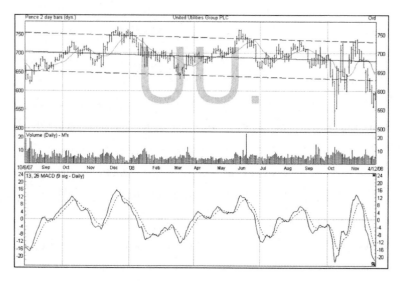

RSI

RSI stands for relative strength indicator. It was devised in 1978 by the American J Welles-Wilder. The intention was for it to address drawbacks in other indicators that tried to measure share price momentum in order to spot possible future turning points. Most momentum indicators aggregate share price differences, or simply the number of 'up' and 'down' days over successive fixed periods of time, usually around ten days to a fortnight.

There is a disadvantage to methods like this. A major share price rise or fall one day might be all well and good. But if prices then show only small increases in subsequent days, in a conventional momentum indicator the signals these methods give will be distorted when the exceptionally large change in price drops out of the calculation.

This is a major flaw when relying on such an indicator to time short-term buying and selling.

The Welles-Wilder RSI calculation gets around this by averaging rather than simply adding the changes on 'up' days and 'down' days

Without going into the detail of the technicalities of the calculation, the RSI typically shows a line that has an upper limit of 100 and a lower limit of zero and which fluctuates quite significantly between these two figures. Typically, the key levels for buying and selling decisions are 30 and 70. If the RSI for a share or index breaks up through the 30 level from below, then that would usually be construed as a buy signal. Similarly if the share or index breaks down through 70 from above, then that is normally a signal to sell.

Chart 7.5: United Utilities RSI

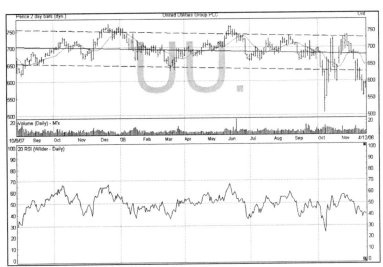

© ShareScope

In the chart of United Utilities, we can see that the RSI has broken up from below the 30 level on one occasion in the recent past. Prior to this we need to go back to the very start of the chart, a year previously, to get another signal of the same type.

Stochastics

As we noted earlier, many technical indicators inevitably only produce convincing signals after the event, so that often some of the benefits of a movement in the share price may have been lost.

Some of the key momentum indicators that attempt to get around this problem are known as stochastic indicators (or simply stochastics). A stochastic pattern is a well known statistical concept observable in many other non-financial situations. In this case, however, stochastics can be particularly effective in establishing turning points in shares which show strong cyclical tendencies.

The idea behind a stochastic indicator is that a share in an uptrend tends to see prices cluster in each successive period at or near the top of the range of prices for that period. The same thing happens in reverse during a downtrend. By representing this on a chart, the turning point in the stochastic value should coincide with, or even precede, the turning point in the underlying security.

The calculation

The stochastic value is calculated by taking the difference between today's price and the low point for the period (say, 15 days) being considered, compared with the difference between the highest and lowest price for the same 15 days. It can therefore vary between zero and 100, the 100 point being reached when today's price is the highest price for the period under consideration, and zero being when it is at the lowest point.

Interpretation

Why does the stochastic work the way it does?

It is mainly because, after a strong rise or fall, prices tend to consolidate. During a period like this, if prices begin to close away from the extreme high or low, the stochastic value will tend to change direction, indicating a potential turning point in the underlying.

So, rather as is the case with the moving averages of share prices, stochastics are of particular significance where divergence occurs in what appear to be major overbought or oversold areas. This might occur, for instance, when the share price rises to close to a new high but the stochastic fails to rise in sympathy. This would be taken as a sell signal. Similarly when the price falls to close to new low but the stochastic doesn't, this could be taken as an imminent buying opportunity.

The way this is highlighted in a chart is for a stochastic value to be smoothed using the average of several periods, with the unsmoothed stochastic value then acting as a trigger when it reverses course by sufficient to cross back over the smoothed average. A technique like this, and other momentum indicators, can be of particular use when trading CFDs.

Chart 7.6: United Utilities Stochastic

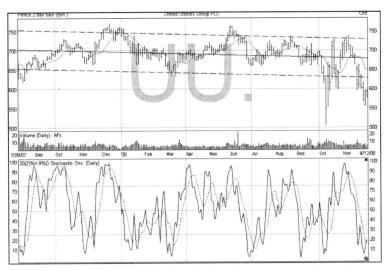

© ShareScope

The trigger effect can be clearly seen in the chart of United Utilities' stochastic oscillator. Compare the lower part of the graph with the upper share price chart to see how the stochastic has signalled turning points.

Charting software

Many years ago, technical analysts used to draw charts by hand. That's no longer necessary. The advantage of cheap computing power and the ability to import large quantities of data over the internet means that computer-based charting has taken over, even to the point of real time prices being available to facilitate trading on even the fastest moving of stock market instruments. CFD traders would do well to think about investing in a chart package that offers real time prices, even though this costs more than the normal end-of-day updated packages.

My own preference is for the simpler option – a chart package that uses end-of-day prices (normally sent by email or downloaded from the web). These are available for £100 or so, or for a low monthly fee. Real time prices are much more expensive than end-of-day ones. They are only worth buying if you are happy to make use of them – sat in front of a dealing screen all day.

Programs

In the past I have used Updata's *Technical Analyst* package, which is a little more expensive than some, but offers a choice of either end-of-day or real time prices, for a monthly fee ranging from £29 to £89 plus VAT. Details of the package are available at www.updata.co.uk. This is quite a sophisticated package, which allows easy toggling between different chart types and time periods.

Less costly options, which I also use regularly, include ShareScope and WinStock's *The Analyst*. ShareScope (www.sharescope.co.uk) is available for a monthly fee for data (£14 a month for end-of-day data, or more – ranging up to £85 a month – for real time). All of the share price charts in this book have been taken from the ShareScope system I use. Winstock's (www.winstock.co.uk) software costs around £129.95 for the package with end-of-day data delivered free by email.

Most CFD brokers provide a charting product for their client free of charge on their websites or built in to the onscreen dealing system with which clients interact. This may be sufficient for the needs of most traders, at least at the outset. But it is worth bearing in mind that some of these products may be relatively basic and more cumbersome to use than a conventional software product. Keen traders may therefore wish to have a standalone real time charting product set up on a separate adjacent computer so that orders can be input and the chart observed on separate screens.

Key points about software

- You need to be able to read price charts to time your trades properly.
- Market timing software can help with CFD trades on indices.
- Some software is free. CFD brokers provide basic charting on their websites
- There is extensive literature on how to interpret charts.

Market timing software

Market timing software is a specific type of investment software that looks purely at technical indicators that are calculated and specifically designed to monitor and predict the course of an index or range of indices. These products tend to be designed to look exclusively at the US market, but since it is easy to trade US markets via the medium of CFDs, these are worthwhile using for anyone contemplating serious trading in index CFDs.

Market timing software takes various forms, but my personal favourite is a package called *Ultra* (www.ultrafs.com), which aggregates the evidence of more than 75 tried and tested technical indicators.

The indicators used fall into several broad categories:

1. Stock market indicators (around 85)
2. Bond market indicators (6)
3. Gold market indicators (7)
4. NASDAQ 100 stock market indicators (13)

Daily data is provided to enable each indicator to be recalculated each day (or week, if the indicator is based on weekly readings) and the current status of the indicator determined. Data is downloaded from a password-protected section of the Ultra website.

The current status of all indicators is given (*buy*, *short*, or *cash*), and the percentage change in the market since the start of the year is also provided. An overall summary on the stock market indicators page shows what percentage of indicators suggest a buy and what percentage a sell. Basic charts are provided for a range of indices, technical indicators and market and economic data. Historical data on the performance of each indicator and fully referenced information on how it is compiled is also given.

How might this be useful to you?

Ultra helps by presenting a consensus view of all of the best historically proven systems. The ones that make the grade are the systems that provide the highest probability of future gain with the minimum level of risk of significant losses – without excessive trading.

Figure 7.7: Ultra's market timing software for the US market

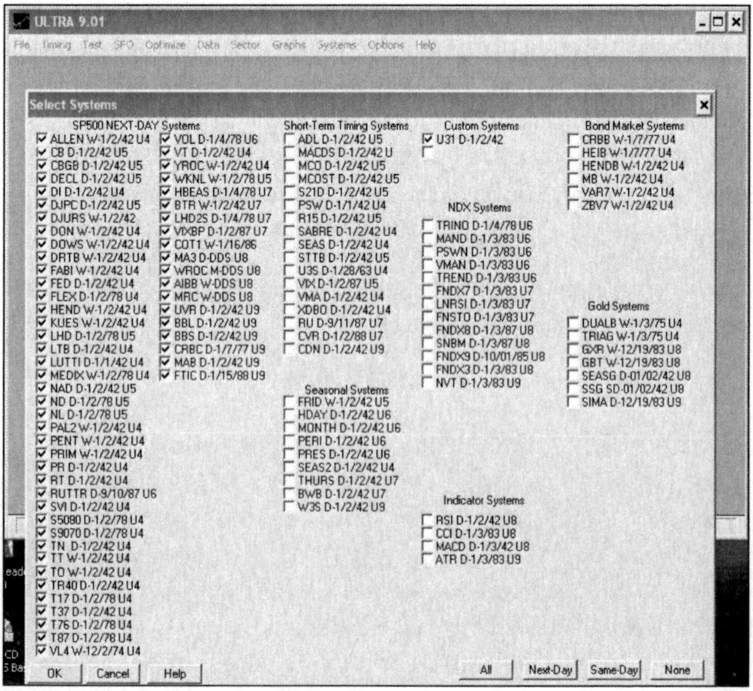

The edge that the Ultra system provides is that each system is tested thoroughly before it is included in the program. About 80% of those investigated are rejected as not being sufficiently durable in all types of market conditions.

The drawback to this system is that no data is available for UK markets. But US markets are easily available through the medium of CFDs. This system is ideal, for example, for trading CFDs on the S&P or NASDAQ indices.

Table 7.2: What software to use and how

Type	Use	Relevant for CFDs?
Chart	Determining scope of trade	Yes
Market timing	Timing buys and sells	Yes (for US indices)

Trading simulators

Interactive Investor has a trade simulation system for clients to trade on a simulated basis. This enables new would-be CFD traders to get a feel for the mechanics of trading CFDs and the degree to which profits and losses can rack up, before starting to trade with real money.

This is an extremely important facility to be able to have and I strongly recommend that anyone new to CFD trading does not deal with a broker that does not offer this facility at the outset. Starting trading and risking real money without some practical indication and experience of the way the market works is courting disaster.

It is particularly important to get practice using an online trading system like this to input order and stop-losses, to close trades, to get a feel for margin requirements, and to view the speed with which the market moves, as well as the costs of trading and how these build up over time.

To see the Interactive Investor Simulator go to www.iii.co.uk/cfd

My recommendation is for would-be clients to trade on a simulated basis for an extended period and to experience at least one or more major daily movements in the overall market (say a daily change of 4% or more) to see how exposed they wish to be to highly leveraged instruments of this sort.

8
Resources for CFD Investors

One of the best aspects of the present-day glut of information available via the internet is that it levels the playing field to some degree for private investors. Dealing can be done online instantly, and there are plenty of resources to help investors negotiate the risks inherent in the market and those specific to individual shares and investment products.

The fact that so much information is available doesn't mean, however, that conventional print sources should be neglected, nor that just because there is lots of data you should leave your brain at home. Thinking about the markets, and making realistic judgements about the potential risks and returns that can be generated by specific trades, is just as important.

This chapter gives a brief resume of some of the best resources available for investors, and specifically those relating directly to or relevant for CFD trading.

Finding the information

Information is power, and you will probably need to read up on the topics relating to trading CFDs in more detail than I have been able to cover in this book. You also need to know where to find price information and other data.

This section looks at web-based sources of information on the topics covered in the previous chapters.

About Interactive Investor

Interactive Investor was born in 1995 and was acquired from AMP by CAPACC (Capital Accumulation Limited) in March 2004, and is headed up by Tomàs Carruthers. CAPACC is also the owner of *Moneywise* and *Money Observer*.

About Interactive Investor

Interactive Investor is the UK's leading personal finance and investment website (www.iii.co.uk). From share dealing to savings, and from ISAs to mortgages, Spread Betting to CFD trading, Interactive Investor provides independent tools and information to enable consumers to address all their investment and personal finance needs. Interactive Investor has 1.6 million registered account holders and 500,000 regular monthly users. Interactive Investor Trading Limited, trading as "Interactive Investor", is authorised and regulated by the Financial Services Authority. *Capacc* acquired Interactive Investor in March 2004.

About Moneywise

Moneywise, first published in 1990, is Britain's best selling personal finance magazine with an ABC audited circulation of 30,151. The magazine is dedicated to presenting financial information in a jargon-free manner dealing with the key financial decisions that everyone needs to consider – from investing for children and buying your first home through to planning for retirement.

The www.moneywise.co.uk website features a wide range of news and tools designed to help people take their first steps on the investment ladder, it includes a dedicated TV channel MoneywiseTV bringing Personal Finance coverage to life for the mass market audience. The new website also provides a range of guides, discussion boards and blogs to guide consumers through the money maze. *Capacc* acquired Money Observer in October 2004.

About Money Observer

Money Observer is the longest established personal finance and investment magazine in the UK, first published 28 years ago, it's a multi-award winning title with an ABC of 23,827. It is the top selling monthly title of its kind on newsstands throughout the UK and is renowned for the depth of analysis it brings to the personal finance and retail investments field. It was founded alongside the *Observer* newspaper. *Capacc* acquired *Money Observer* in February 2008.

Interactive Investor provides the following trading platforms:

CFDs

- 24 Hour Online and Telephone trading platform allowing you to trade markets around the world
- NO Commission on Index & Sector CFDs
- NO Commission on Forex, Gold & Silver CFDs
- LOW Commission on Equity CFDs - trade from £15
- Stop losses and guaranteed stop losses
- Powerful technical analysis and charting tools
- Trade Simulator

Spread Betting

- 24 Hour Online and Telephone trading platform allowing you to trade markets around the world
- NO Commission charges
- Stop losses and guaranteed stop losses
- Powerful technical analysis and charting tools
- Trade Simulator
- Free Financial Spread Betting Handbook when you place your first trade

Share Dealing

- Buy shares for £1.50 using Portfolio Builder
- £10 flat fee for real-time UK trades
- £15 flat fee for US and European trades
- Trade Shares, Investment Trusts & ETFs
- Transfer your share certificates to us FREE
- TradePlan service

Funds

- Hold shares, funds or cash within your ISA
- Save up to 100% on initial fund charges
- Our regular flexible investment plan – Funds Builder
- Save up to 100% on initial fund charges
- Over 1600 funds, over 70 fund managers
- No account administration or inactivity fees
- Fully Self-Select ISA (funds & shares)
- Fund and stock filter tools

Sipp

- Hold funds, shares, cash and bonds
- Same, low-cost transaction charges
- No set-up fees for new accounts
- Low annual administration fee
- Over 1600 funds, over 70 fund managers
- Save up to 100% on initial fund charges
- Commission costs from just £1.50 in shares

Software

I have indicated which of the sites mentioned in previous sections have trading simulators or other valuation tools. It may be, however, that you want to use stand-alone software that can be downloaded to your PC.

Sharescope

Sharescope's extensive system encompasses both sophisticated technical analysis indicators and charts, and also detailed fundamental data on companies, including a data-mining facility for screening stocks for particular fundamental and valuation attributes. Further details are at www.sharescope.co.uk.

Updata

Updata's *Technical Analyst* is an excellent general technical analysis package. Further details of this software can be found at www.updata.co.uk.

Ultra

I have mentioned market timing software like *Ultra* (www.ultrafs.com), which is a useful aid to trading CFDs on US index related products.

Books

Note: in the following the code referred to is that used by the Interactive Investor Bookshop (www.iii.co.uk).

General

The following are mini-reviews of a selection of books that will allow you to read more on derivatives in general and the particular categories of product you might wish to deal in. I recommend further reading before you take the plunge.

An Introduction to Derivatives
John Wiley, 1999

A beginner's guide to derivatives which includes definitions, descriptions, quizzes and examples. Futures, options and swaps are studied from basic concepts through to applications in trading, hedging and arbitrage.

Derivatives – The Wild Beast of Finance
Alfred Steinherr
John Wiley, 2000

The second edition of a book first published in spring 1998 in which the author predicted a destabilisation of the global market structure if some firm risk management were not exercised in the derivatives market. His predictions became reality and this edition brings the story up to date. The role of derivatives in a developing world economy is discussed at length in a lively and informative manner. The final part of the book looks into the future and predicts the exportation of the American model of finance to the rest of the world. (Code 12533)

Against the Gods
Peter L. Bernstein
John Wiley, 1996

The story of risk from gamblers in ancient Greece to modern chaos theory. The author explains the concepts of probability, sampling, regression, game theory, and rational versus irrational decision making while exploring the role of risk in modern society. Character sketches of world-renowned intellects such as Pascal and Bernoulli and Bayes and Keynes are included as well as the stories of inspired amateurs who influenced modern thinking. The general topic of risk is tied into risk management and thereby to derivatives. (Code 9734)

Fooled by Randomness (The Hidden Role of Chance in the Markets and in Life)
Nassim Nicholas Taleb
Penguin Books Ltd, 2007

This is an exploration of how people perceive and deal with luck in business and life. Three major intellectual issues are discussed; the problem of induction, the survivorship biases; and our genetic unfitness to the modern world. Numerous characters who have grasped the significance of chance appear in the book such as George Soros and philosopher Karl Popper. (Code 168556)

See also Nassim Taleb's more recent book, *The Black Swan* (Penguin 2007), about the role of random events that are hugely influential but impossible to predict.

Bear Market Investing Strategies
Harry D. Schultz
John Wiley, 2002

The book aims to provide the necessary tools for an investor to survive in a bear market. In addition bear markets are looked at from a historical viewpoint, together with the structure and economic conditions in which they thrive. (Code 14919)

Inventing Money (Long Term Capital Management and the Search for Risk-Free Profits)
Nick Dunbar
John Wiley, 1999

This is an account of the events leading up to the collapse of the hedge fund LTCM. It provides an insight into the world of arbitrage and derivatives. The book tells the story of the individuals and institutions involved and analyses in detail the trades and the reasons why they went wrong. (Code 14738)

Come Into my Trading Room
Dr Alexander Elder
Wiley Trading, 2002

As befits an author who is a professional psychiatrist as well as a professional trader and expert in technical analysis the book deals with the mind as well as method. It is aimed at beginners but contains useful information for all levels of trading experience. It considers the overall management of money, time and strategy necessary for successful trading. (Code 14556)

45 Years In Wall Street
W.D.Gann
Lambert Gann, 1949

Although written over fifty years ago the book contains valuable rules for investing which still apply today together with charts for determining stock trends. This is aimed at the experienced investor and draws on the author's forty-five years of trading experience. (Code 269728)

Elliott Wave Principle – 20th Anniversary Edition
Robert Prechter and Alfred Frost
New Classics Library,1998

This is a basic handbook explaining the theory and application of Elliott Wave. (Code 9944)

Investment Psychology Explained
Martin Pring
Wiley, 1993

The main idea of this book is not to let emotions interfere with investment decisions. The author draws from his own experience and from the collective wisdom of many well-known investors such as Bernard Baruch and Humphrey Neill. (Code 0985)

Technical Analysis

Technical Analysis Plain and Simple
Michael N. Kahn
FT Prentice Hall, 1999

A beginner's guide to chart reading explaining the terminology, theories, risks and application of technical analysis. (Code 23768)

Dynamic Technical Analysis
Philippe Cahen
Wiley Trading, 2001

The book concentrates on the use of the analytical technique of Bollinger bands. Written by a professional trader, it is aimed at the experienced investor with charting knowledge. (Code 14270)

Beyond Technical Analysis
Tushar S. Chande
Wiley Trading, 2001

A comprehensive guide on the use of technical analysis to build up investment strategies in both the stock and futures markets, and one that is useful for CFDs too. A useful section for the beginner covers the basics of technical analysis but the book is primarily aimed at those familiar with the techniques who wish to develop their skills further.

Millard on Channel Analysis
Brian J. Millard
Wiley, 1997

This explains the technique of channel analysis. This identifies cycles in share price movements. The book illustrates how using this method to predict the stock market together with a strict disciplined approach can help investors. It is aimed at those with a prior knowledge of charting techniques.

Millard on Profitable Charting Techniques
Brian J. Millard
Wiley, 1997

Practical guide to using charts and indicators.

Technical Analysis of the Financial Markets
John J. Murphy
New York Institute of Finance, 1999

An invaluable, comprehensive guide to charts and charting by an author with over 30 years experience of applying technical analysis. Written in a clear, logical style with over 400 real-life charts to clarify the points raised. (Code 10044)

Trading Classic Chart Patterns
Thomas N. Bulkowski
Wiley Trading, 2002

Written by a successful full-time investor, the book is divided into two sections. The first, aimed at the novice, explains the basics of investing and technical analysis. The second part consists of a chart pattern reference section arranged alphabetically, together with a scoring system for each pattern and case studies. (Code 14723)

The Day Trader's Guide to Technical Analysis
Clive Lewis
McGraw-Hill Professional, 2000

This is aimed at traders who are already familiar with charts and charting and illustrates how they can be incorporated into the day trading environment.

Point and Figure Charting
Thomas Dorsey
Wiley, 2001

A classic step-by-step source on the subject but brought up-to-date by incorporating recent software developments. (Code 146796)

The Definitive Guide to Point & Figure Charting
Jeremy du Plessis
Harriman House, 2005

Does exactly what it says on the cover, providing a guide to this key technical analysis discipline from a doyen among chartists and creator of market leading technical analysis software. (Code 21822)

Encyclopedia of Chart Patterns
Thomas Bulkowski
John Wiley, 2000

A comprehensive practical guide to over 50 chart formations. (Code 21437)

Technical Analysis Applications in the Global Currency Markets
Cornelius Luca
McGraw-Hill Professional, 2004

Written by a foreign exchange currency expert the book shows how technical analysis can be applied to foreign exchange trading via the medium of CFDs, although the methods used are not necessarily specific to the FX market. (Code 19982)

The Investors Chronicle Guide to Charting
Alistair Blair
FT Prentice Hall, 2002

This is aimed at the private investor with no previous charting experience. Charting theories are explained in detail using purpose-drawn charts and worked examples. One section is devoted to applying the technique to recent (at that time) share price charts for each of the top FTSE companies.

Technical Analysis and Stock Market Profits
Richard Schabacker
Harriman House, 2005

Written by one of the founders of modern technical analysis. This is a major text on the subject that was first published in 1932 and was originally intended as a practical investment course. The basic techniques explored still apply today. (Code 21482)

Head and Shoulder Tops
David Schwartz and Robin Griffiths
Burleigh Publishing, 1997

A booklet aimed at avoiding trading losses by identifying these distinctive patterns. (Code 4958)

Chart Reading for Professional Traders
Michael S.Jenkins
Traders Press, 1996

According to the author the book attempts to demonstrate the principles of chart reading and technical analysis as applied to general chart reading for trading purposes. By these means he hopes to help traders make profits consistently. (Code 9807)

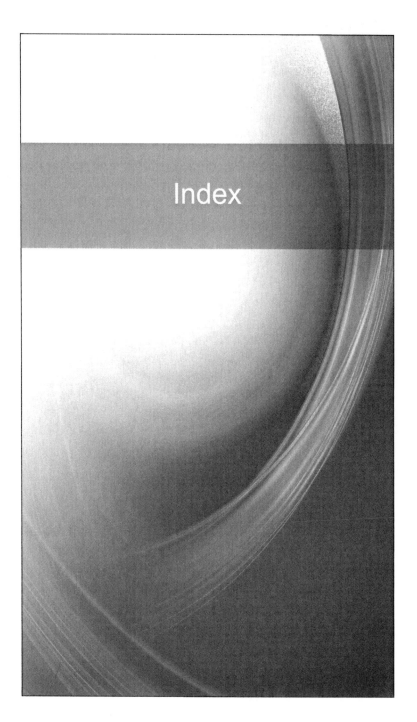

Index

A

asset allocation strategy 91-93
AstraZeneca 120-121

B

Barclays 19
Barclays Capital's Equity-Gilt Study 6
bear market 4-5, 7
bibliography 139-145
bid-offer spread 35, 43, 56-57, 66, 80, 95
    pairs trading 77
BP 19
broker(s) viii, 21, 23, 24, 24, 32-33, 38, 39, 41, 50-60, 107-108, 128
    application 51-52
    commission 25, 33-36, 43, 54, 58
    differences between firms 25, 33, 38-40, 43, 46, 54
    directory of 136.137
    execution-only 36, 43, 59-60
    interest 54
bubbles 4
bull market 4-5
buy and hold 7, 101

C

Cable & Wireless 95
capital gains tax (CGT) 7, 25, 29, 34, 49, 53, 87, 88, 89, 90, 110, 111
cash extraction 73-76
cash settlement 11, 14
CFDs see contracts for difference
CGT see capital gains tax
commission 25, 33-36, 43, 58

commission free trading 43, 54
    pairs trading 77
confidence intervals see confidence limits
confidence limit(s) 122-123
contract(s) 13-14, 21, 29, 32, 33, 53, 57-58
    futures 14
    hedging 17
    open ended (no expiry time) 32
    selling short 24
contracts for difference (CFDs)
    basic characteristics 7-8, 30-34
    buying/selling contracts 13
    complementary part of your investing 41
    dealing specifics 53
    experience, importance of vii, 39, 51-2, 59, 95, 116, 131-132
    definition 13, 31-32
    flexibility 7, 13, 86
    gear(ing) 15-16, 21, 29, 31, 42, 43, 45-46, 63, 109-110
        risks 15, 67
    hedging vii, 17
        strategy 87-90
    long trade example 35-36
    mathematics 35
    no time limit 115
    risk viii, 23, 39, 56, 58, 104
        gearing 45-46
        managing 3, 15, 41, 42, 107, 110-111
            strategy, using to manage 68-72, 77-82, 83-86

I

Index Gold (IG) 6

indices

    CAC40 18

    comparing key features 20

    DAX 18

    Dow Jones Industrial Average (DJIA)18,107

    FTSE 100 5, 14, 18, 19, 107

        relative value trade 83-86

    NASDAQ 100 102, 129, 131

    S&P500 18, 22, 120, 131

interest rates 14, 41, 46, 54-55, 59, 79, 115, 119

internet resources 136-138

L

Leeson, Nick 3

LIBOR see London Inter Bank Offered Rate

London Inter Bank Offered Rate (LIBOR) 54-55

London Stock Exchange dividend calculator 94

Long Term Capital Management 3

M

MACD see moving average convergence divergence

margin 13, 15, 16, 21, 23, 31, 39-40, 53, 55-56, 65, 73-74, 82, 96, 109

    initial margin 21, 38, 40, 43

    gearing 29, 65, 67

    margin calls 39, 74-75, 99, 105

rates of, comparative 56

trading simulators 131

typical rates in CFDs 40

variation margin 21

volatility 22, 38

Marks & Spencer (M&S) 122-123

money management 104-106, 121

moving average 117, 121, 123, 127

Moving Average Convergence Divergence (MACD) 123-124

M&S see Marks and Spencer

O

options 3, 11, 14, 18

    comparison with other derivatives 25, 32-34, 53, 55, 86

    definition 13

    margin 40

    private options traders 42

    stop-loss(es) 42

    time limit 50

    volatility 22

P

pairs trading 41, 77-82

patterns 118

    head and shoulders pattern 120

R

recommended reading 139-145

relative strength indicator (RSI) 124-125

reversion to the mean 4, 5

risk viii, 23, 39, 56, 58

    gearing 45-46